Motherhood Redeemed

MOTHERHOOD REDEEMED

How Radical Feminism
Betrayed Maternal Love

Kimberly Cook

TAN Books
Gastonia, North Carolina

Cover design by Caroline Green

Cover image by TairA / Shutterstock

Library of Congress Control Number: 2020942442

ISBN: 978-1-5051-1648-9
Kindle ISBN: 978-1-5051-1649-6
EPUB ISBN: 978-1-5051-1650-2

Published in the United States by
TAN Books
PO Box 269
Gastonia, NC 28053
www.TANBooks.com

Printed in the United States of America

To Cory, whose love and masculine virtue has encouraged me to discover my own authentic feminine genius

"A woman's soul . . . is also fashioned to be a shelter in which other souls may unfold. Both spiritual companionship and spiritual motherliness are not limited to the physical wife and mother relationship, but they extend to all people with whom woman comes into contact."[1]

—St. Teresa Benedicta (Edith Stein)

---

[1] Edith Stein, *Essays on Woman*, vol. II (Washington, D.C.: ICS Publications, 2017), 132.

Contents

Introduction

The pain of motherhood is a cleansing fire. I experience this each time I birth a child, a true phenomenon of hanging on the precipice between life and death. In one moment, I'm recalling the pain and horror of being cast out of the Garden of Eden as my body trembles in the pain of childbirth. In the very next moment, as I hold my newborn child, I'm being ushered into the sweet relief of heavenly glory. There is no moment on earth like the moment of giving birth for a mother. Likewise, there are no tears to compare with those wept from the eyes of a mother who has lost her child in this lifetime.

A woman's motherhood is not limited to the physical sphere. The heart of our nation has long been shaped by women who were driven to respond to the concerns afflicting humanity. Great women—though not always immortalized in history books—have come forth from every generation, demographic, and race to challenge injustice, fight for freedom, and uphold truth, goodness, and beauty. When women are allowed the space to assert themselves and nurture those they love, their full potential can be reached. Throughout history, many women were not given the freedom to assert themselves. Currently, women feel they must hide their nurturing gifts or divorce them from their work.

One of the greatest betrayals of women in today's American culture is the deconstruction and denial of their physical and spiritual maternity. Women are put at enmity with their bodies and their sex: pregnancy is a disease to be avoided, and children are its curse. As one of the leading American women of the nineteenth-century women's movement, Elizabeth Cady Stanton, said, "Wonder not that American women do everything in their power to avoid maternity; for, from false habits of life, dress, food, and generations of disease and abominations, it is to them a period of sickness, lassitude, disgust, agony and death."[2] In the twenty-first century, women not only avoid physical maternity but shrink from embracing their spiritual maternity as well. This is their immense capacity of self-gift and an acceptance of others that brings unity and peace to the human family.

We'll see how the suffragettes and abolitionists decried American patriarchy for robbing women of their personhood and reducing humanity to mere possession. For many, patriarchy became the enemy of justice, and even religion seemed to champion female oppression. This has paved the way for relativism and led masculinity to become defined by culture instead of divine revelation.

But who are we as women in the eyes of God? Where is the Christian woman's place in the history of activism and the fight for her freedom and rights? How does our immeasurable maternal influence continue to echo throughout the chapters of American history?

---

2   Elizabeth Cady Stanton, "Infanticide and Prostitution," *The Revolution*, vol. I, no. 5, February 5, 1868.

I seek to illuminate the inseparable union of maternity—both biological and spiritual—and women. Motherhood extends beyond biological children and is the highest expression of femininity. As the great twentieth-century Jewish philosopher and Catholic convert St. Teresa Benedicta (Edith Stein) said, "Both spiritual companionship and spiritual motherliness are not limited to the physical wife and mother relationship, but they extend to all people with whom woman comes into contact."[3] Stein said that "no woman is only *woman*," and regardless of her "individual specialty and talent," her feminine nature offers something to the world that the male nature *cannot*.

This book weaves my personal experience of radical feminism with an overview of key points in the American feminism movement. By sharing my personal encounter, the reader will hopefully gain a balanced understanding of the leading feminists and philosophies of the movement. I also challenge the deconstruction of conception, sex, and gender while defending the great vocation of women, as upheld by the teachings of the Catholic Church.

Feminism was my rebellion against conformity and my expression to the world that I didn't need anyone's approval to dissent from traditional perceptions of women. It exuded power and resounded a unified female voice throughout history, which I came to discover wasn't quite so unified. It also further removed me from embracing my innate feminine reality. This isn't to discount the many goods rightly

---

[3]   Edith Stein, *Essays on Woman*, vol. II (Washington, DC: ICS Publications, 2017), 132.

won for the freedom of women—continuously ending their undue oppression—but so few of these causes are justifiably exclusive to an unbiased feminism. The threads of feminism have been woven with harmful ideologies concerning women's bodies, reproduction and participation in marriage and family life. Women have been influenced to reject both their nature and feminine virtue in the most vehement manner. When feminism was left unanswered, it allowed us to slide into our current cultural reality, in which you can't question non-binary gender without being labelled an unenlightened transphobic or a bigot.

As I became more influenced by feminist philosophies, I rejected both government and religion. A disdain for motherhood began to develop within me, especially for women who sacrificed their education and career for the sake of motherhood. But worse than that was my own potential as a woman to undergo such a curse. I saw every pregnancy as a crisis pregnancy. Near the end of my involvement in the feminist movement and close to my own ruin, I discovered how the influence of feminism had deformed my soul. I became a disciple of St. John Paul the Great's writings on the dignity of women and the feminine *genius*: the unique predisposition women have toward spiritual intuition, sensitivity, generosity, and fidelity. It was then that I knew what I was truly fighting against: a better version of myself, the woman God had created me to be.

For a long period of time, I believed that I could never be married or have children because of the residue of my disdain for motherhood, which might still lurk in the crevices of my soul. Discovering God's love and wanting to serve him regardless of my woundedness, I considered a religious vocation where I could learn to love with maternal abandon. My fierce dedication to serve women was elevated through my faith and allowed me to participate in the healing work of many women. I went into the wilderness of Wyoming to serve young women deemed "hopeless" by their families and the justice system. I counseled and fought for women in Washington, DC, who were pregnant and often alone (many poor immigrants without basic means, medical access, or support). I taught students from many diverse backgrounds and shared the joys and sorrows of their young lives as I worked to get my master's degree in theology.

To my great surprise, God did call me to marriage and to motherhood, my hardest and most rewarding task. Through motherhood, I encounter my ugliest vices as well as the elevated beauty of each human soul. Motherhood has unlocked the simple truth that love is not divided but rather multiplied. Every sacrifice, talent, and gift I have to offer is better because I am a mother. Now I work with God in becoming the best version of myself as I grapple with the awesome vocation of being entrusted with souls that are not my own.

It is no wonder that images like the Pietà and meditations of Jesus's mother at the foot of the cross affect us so deeply. In experiencing the great suffering of loss through miscarriage, my heart was consumed with an emptiness that seemed impossible to overcome. The love that I had for my child who was not yet born, but whom I carried in my body, was sacred. It was as real as the true hidden presence of Jesus in the tabernacle. Through the loss of that child, my body ached for the pains of pregnancy and the labor that would bring that sweet child into my arms. I longed to smile across the room at her rejoicing father as he held her for the first time. This is how I know that love is not a curse, that motherhood is not an imposition of nature on the bodies of women, and that all things have an eternal gravity that cannot be denied, ignored, or circumvented.

Kimberly Cook

PART ONE

The Genesis of Feminism

What Is Feminism?

"With centuries of degradation, we have so little of true womanhood, that the world has but the faintest glimmering of what a woman is or should be."[4]

—*The Revolution*, 1869

At the heart of feminism is an authentic quest for the true nature of womanhood. Starting from any place other than in conversation with our Creator leaves us without meaningful answers and provides only shadowy outlines of what femininity is meant to be. We are tempted to deny or distort our femininity, either competing with masculinity or consuming media that diminishes women to vapid, conniving, and promiscuous archetypes. Worse than this objectification is watching women objectify their own bodies for the sake of political statements and radical attention-grabbing stunts. The true nature of womanhood is a supernatural vision of beauty. It is not the artificially perfected images in magazines but the radical, objective radiance that delights the soul to such a depth of shining clarity that it moves others to embrace its divine source.[5]

---

[5] Donald DeMarco, "Can Beauty Save the World?" *Lay Witness*, November/December, 2009, 16-17.

At the heart of all humanity is a desire for love. My own heart is no different. So how did a tomboy with a limitless imagination, who liked adventure, as well as to accessorize, become a feminist? Well, I will tell you. It was through a series of influences and events, most of which could have gone either way. A defining, yet still surreal, season of my life was spent playing in a female punk band for many years. Our faithful roadies would be onstage assembling our band equipment and tuning instruments as we surveyed the crowd from the dark and smoky backstage. Drinks were free for musicians and drugs were plentiful. One memorable night in Baltimore, I kept my eyes focused ahead of me, pretending not to notice the guy snorting a line of cocaine off the pool table as I walked past. My exterior had to remain stoic to survive in this business, and it took everything to keep the band alive (literally).

Strapping my guitar across my black dress and walking the length of the stage to the microphone, I nervously absorbed the packed little room bursting with energy. Turning for a nod of confidence from my drummer, whose wild curly hair hung down over her tattooed shoulders, I slammed out the first note and began forcefully pouring angry lyrics into the mic. The crowd began to churn and tumble in the chaos of our amplified lament. This was but one of many nights spent onstage, traveling across the country in our tour van, or flying to an overseas festival. I was often the only "straight girl" in our all-girl punk band, and although I always had boyfriends, I was one of the few not "experimenting" with my sexuality among our friends and fellow musicians.

Exploiting sexuality was part of the experience, and it was encouraged in the coming-of-age drama as a rocker on the road to enlightenment. But where did that "enlightenment" get us? At the end of many years on stage, I recalled the bandmates and friends who had fallen to serious depression and suicide. Some had attempted self-harm and others were institutionalized. Many were still chasing one drug addiction after another. Somehow, at the end of it, I was the only one not addicted to a serious narcotic. However, I *was* addicted to something much stronger: rebellion, and that disease was deep in my soul.

Despite its pain and darkness, I could not help being in love with the feminist punk movement, its fierceness in bringing to life the angry literary and historic heroines and the lament of irrepressible injustices. I adopted their philosophies and their purpose became my purpose. I was fueled by an explosive cocktail of my fiery teenage angst, an unquenchable curiosity, the loss of my religion, and the right combination of people to stoke the flames of my conversion to the cause.

However, it did not start that way. As a girl, my badges of honor were the skinned knees proving that I had challenged myself to climb the tallest trees and my eyes blazed with excitement constructing forts of fallen limbs and overhanging tree branches. I was raised to love the outdoors and be as self-sufficient as a modern girl could be. Greeted each morning by the framed picture of Annie Oakley displayed on my dresser, I learned to shoot a rifle and repel down the side of mountains by the time I was a first grader. Some of my fondest childhood memories are of afternoons spent in the creeks by my house, chasing the stream barefoot with my friends for miles as it hopped over the smooth rocks of creek beds. There was no end to our exploration nor season that would stop us; each night as darkness set in the sky, I could be found racing back home full of mud and imagination from those wild little adventures.

Aside from one or two treasured childhood girlfriends, I was surrounded almost entirely by boys. Thankfully, I blended in just as well with them, and calculating the amount of freedom boys seemed to have compared to girls, I often wondered if I would be better off as a boy. Then again, I wasn't really missing out on anything as a girl. My parents allowed me the freedom to be a girl who liked doing a lot of the things that boys liked to do. They never questioned my sexuality or pushed me into a ladylike box. I never saw counselors or medical doctors to discuss my gender identity or early sex changes and hormone treatment plans. In fact, I never really thought about gender at all back then. Gender was as foreign to me as adulthood.

My mother voted in all elections alongside my father. She went to college and eventually opened her own business. My parents seemed to be equal in marriage, although my dad worked outside of the home and my mom chose to stay at home with my brother and me. I grew up in a microcosm of modern lower middle-class American society, unaware that women had ever known any less.

But the truth is that women have known significantly less. Those early American activists, who are sometimes considered to be part of the first wave of feminism, fought many fierce years of political and social battles in order to be recognized as citizens with equal rights. Their efforts were not clouded by the desire to *be* men but rather to be fully women—free to pursue the same social and political opportunities as men without having to masquerade as men. Woman's rights pioneer Elizabeth Cady Stanton wrote, "I have such an intense pride of sex that the triumphs of woman in art, literature, oratory, science, or song rouse my enthusiasm as nothing else can."[6] It's because of these *distinct* values that femininity affords the family *and* society that the earliest activists fought so vehemently for equality of education, marital rights, and a political voice.

Were the early activists feminists? That's debatable. In truth, we can't answer that question without knowing what feminism is, and that isn't an easy task. As American philosopher Janet Smith soberly put it, "There are almost as many brands of feminism as there are feminists."[7] So then, what *is* feminism? Who *can* define it? Is it a label, philosophy, ideology, political strategy, civil rights movement, or simply an ambiguous power play setting us further apart from men, often with hostility?

To say "feminism is complicated" would be an understatement. Its four "waves" rushed over the landscape of American liberty, separated by time periods, each accompanied by its own political, cultural, and academic beliefs. Each wave

---

[6] Elizabeth Cady Stanton, *Eighty Years and More: Reminiscences 1815–1897* (New York: European Publishing Company, 1898), 263.

[7] Janet Smith, "Feminism, Motherhood, and the Church," in *Proceedings of the Wethersfield Institute*, vol. 3 *The Catholic Woman*, ed. Ralph McInerny (Ignatius Press, 1990), 43.

was ambitious for change. Half of all feminists find the progression of its waves to be a corrosive hijacking of its original principles. Meanwhile, the other half applaud the continued efforts won by the movement and victoriously wave its flag in testament to meeting the cultural needs of women in our changing society. It's arguable that although feminism originally derived from the need to secure equal and fair rights for women in society, who at the time were not recognized as legitimate American citizens, the fight didn't stop with suffrage, and instead transmuted into a battleground over contraception, abortion, and gender.

When we, as twenty-first-century Americans, think of feminism, our memories hardly go back as far as the nineteenth century, when early fighters for women's rights arose: the bold and lucid Susan B. Anthony and Elizabeth Cady Stanton, whose original accomplishments are overshadowed by the flaunted moral decay of their successors, including women such as Margaret Sanger, who introduced birth control and Planned Parenthood; Simone de Beauvoir, who denied gender and despised maternity; Betty Friedan, the founder and first president of the *National Organization for Women*; Gloria Steinem, the leading frontwoman of *Ms.* magazine; and Helen Gurley Brown, the outrageous editor-in-chief of *Cosmopolitan*. These women dominated the *Sexual Revolution* of the '60s and '70s by pushing the social envelope to embrace abortion and homosexuality while attacking the American housewife.

Hot on their heels were the third-wave feminists of the '80s and '90s, fighting for the (re)construction of gender and medical advancements in contraception and in vitro fertilization. These feminists proudly continued the fight for reproductive rights without limitations and ushered in feminism's fourth wave around 2012, championing gender fluidity and unrestricted sexual experimentation and bodily self-determination.

Today's feminism embraces terms such as "fluid," "progressive," and "relative." This hardly allows for anything more than a gender-specific bias to separate it from the doctrine of relativism, which holds that there are no absolutes. Instead, all applicable knowledge, truth, and morality are formed and defined by our current American culture. Feminism is accused of pushing the cultural standard in striving to break the social norms of each generation; first politically, then socially, and now medically. What are the absolutes?

Feminists do agree on one thing: equal opportunities and rights for women. But, unfortunately, the definition of "equal" has also been muddied. Feminists are at war with each other over the definition of women's "rights." This has arguably been a bloody business when it comes to abortion. Even the understanding of the definition of "woman" itself separates modern feminists into fragments. Somewhere along the quest for the true nature of womanhood, the question changed from what *is* feminism to what *is* a woman?

Woman Scorned

I challenge you to do justice in considering the disenfranchised women of the past. This is considerably difficult for our modern society, steeped in gender confusion and a complete lack of propriety. We are tempted to place our female predecessors somewhere between the romantic dam-sels of fairytales and hateful women at war with their own sex. The pioneers of the women's movement did not despise their gender but rather disdained their unwelcomed place in progressing society, as women. Rising anger is detected and recorded and cannot be ignored from the pens of many prominent and lesser-known women who suffered the injus-tice of being women in a society which both pretentiously respected and, in the same turn, completely disregarded her.

Humanity must seek to develop and not abolish or threaten our distinct feminine and masculine natures. Women and men cannot be defined by *what* they do rather than *who* they are, and production should never become humanity's crowning achievement. Although some early and prominent women's rights activists abandoned Christianity for Unitar-ian and agnostic beliefs, compromised the suffrage of other minorities, and opened doors to the breakdown rather than rebuilding of the family, we must face women's battle for social freedom head-on and examine the chapters of femi-nine history that have led us to the feminism of today.

I challenge you to see women as mothers—of men, philosophies, theologies, and inventions. To value their maternal gifts as unique and sacred: in the home as well as the public sphere. Women must never be divided from their motherhood or be made to prove their equality with men in the accomplishment of every task (natural and material). Women derive their power from their inseparable feminine and maternal nature, endowed by their Creator, and through which they accomplish many great things.

The Division of Self

As women began entering the workforce and demanding equality from their employers, the key strategist in the nineteenth-century woman's movement, Susan B. Anthony, advised women to make their employers understand "that you are in their service as workers, not as women."[8] This telling phrase demonstrates how working women had to divide themselves in becoming either a "worker" *or* a "woman" in their place of work. Women were not valued for the contributions of both their feminine nature and their work interdependently in the public sphere.

With the help of the Industrial Revolution's machine-operated inventions, the following century more readily accepted women into the workforce, but not simultaneously as mothers. It wasn't until the Pregnancy Discrimination Act of 1978 that it became illegal to fire, demote, or refuse to hire a woman for being pregnant.

While the twenty-first century has welcomed the female worker, who is both woman and mother, social confusion has tumultuously grown over her balanced obligation to family and society. These stages of confusion have contributed to the rejection and misunderstanding of our distinct human nature as women and men. We find ourselves continually stumbling, either in circles or toward God.

I also floundered for many years between stumbling in circles and toward God—at times using history as an alibi and at others as a piercing weapon. Although many of the

---

[8] Ida Husted Harper, *The Life and Work of Susan B. Anthony*, vol. I (Indianapolis: The Hollenbeck Press, 1898), 308.

doors previously closed to my female predecessors have never been closed to me, I remember vividly an incident from my childhood when, for the first time, I was rejected on account of *not* being a boy.

By the age of seven, it seemed normal to me to be the only girl in my group of childhood friends. Due to the shortage of girls in our neighborhood and only having a brother, the options were simple: isolation or co-education! To their credit, I was treated as an equal by the boys in everything from backyard sports to bike races alike. Few differences were considered between us, other than always having to play the one female G.I. Joe character, Scarlett, and in so doing, often having to remain at "base" on counter-intelligence rather than meeting the real action in the field.

But on one hot summer afternoon a few years later, a boy from the adjoining neighborhood made his way across the field to challenge our rag-tag gang to a baseball showdown. All the customary elements of taunting and teasing were present as the arrangements were made and the boy retreated to gather his team. Adrenalin begun pumping through my veins as I ran home with my brother to grab our bat and mitts. Less than a half hour later our awkward prepubescent team stood behind proud proclamations of victory as we marched onto the field adjoining our two neighborhoods.

The other boys were mostly older and rougher and looked like giants compared to us. I began to shrink back inside of myself as they scanned our sorry team, their eyes plainly resting on me. One boy laughed at the sight of me and broadcasted mockingly, "You brought a girl? There are no girls allowed in baseball." Then turning to me, he sneered, "Go home and play with your dolls!" As his teammates erupted in fits of laughter, I could feel the boys on my team getting hot down the line next to me. The mouthiest boy on our side began hurling every sort of insult back as retaliation, oddly and crassly defending my honor. I remember him shouting, "She can play better than any of you, any day of the week!"

I wanted to run away, but I knew that I couldn't. The future respect of all girls in this neighborhood depended on me and on this moment (or so it seemed). "Alright," the bully menacingly consented. "*I'll* pitch the ball to her, and we'll see if she can hit it or not." I was trapped! All eyes were on me. Amid affirming nods and grumbles of accord, we agreed the challenge was fair, and as thankful as I was for my team's confidence in me, I nervously stepped up to the bat. In that moment I was alone on the sandlot with the setting sun behind the rooftops in the distance. My personal and team pride weighed heavily upon me as the wind passing through the field was the only sound.

Their pitcher wound his arm and smirked at me as I drew a strong and steady breath. I glued my eyes to that ball and said a prayer as I swung the bat harder than I had ever swung before. The reverberation of metal from the bat ran up my arms, causing them to ache as it contacted the ball and I quickly let it fall to the ground. There was an eruption of cheering behind me, and I looked up through the rays of sun to watch my ball sail above the heads of the shocked boys with their mouths gaping open in the outfield. There seemed to be nothing but silence in the field for quite a while, until at last the pitcher spoke up; "She's on our team!" he loudly pronounced, trying to save face, and then he said no more.

This was a defining moment for me, one in which I became soberly aware of just how different I was from my male peers. Despite their acceptance of me, this chasm continued to become greater with age, and I found myself pressured to prove myself time and again on account of my gender. The constant challenge of coming-of-age as a girl among boys became exhausting and confusing. Although I wasn't limited from playing with them or required to stay home and do housework, I wondered what my defining difference was. Nothing at all was required of me, except to grow into a happy and healthy member of society. I could vote, join the workforce, publish radical philosophical papers, influence crowds of free-thinkers, and ultimately change the world.

Original Cause

Only one hundred years ago, my defining difference would have been my membership in the "delicate" sex, making me—in the eyes of men and greater society—unfit for matters of business and government. My only place would have been in the private sphere, which may have brought marital bliss or hostile domestic suffering. Either way, my property and children would not have been my own in marriage and even my identity would have been absorbed into my husband's.

When the fathers of this country prophetically argued that man, government, and society would crumble and oppress one another without a moral and just foundation, they discounted the sentiments of women such as eighteenth-century English writer and radical philosopher Mary

Wollstonecraft. She said, "If [women] be not prepared by education to become the companion of man, she will stop the progress of knowledge, for truth must be common to all. . . . And how can woman be expected to co-operate, unless she know why she ought to be virtuous?"[9]

To be accurate, a woman's participation in government was *considered*, although unchallenged at the foundation of the United States of America. In May of 1776, the second president, John Adams, wrote a letter to James Sullivan concerning the principles of representation under a moral government:

> How, then, does the right arise in the majority to govern the minority, against their will? Whence arises the right of the men to govern the women, without their consent? . . . But why exclude women? You will say, because their delicacy renders them unfit for practice and experience in the great businesses of life, and the hardy enterprises of war, as well as the arduous cares of state. Besides, their attention is so much engaged with the necessary nurture of their children, that nature has made them fittest for domestic cares. And children have not judgment or will of their own. True. But will not these reasons apply to others . . . too dependent upon other men to have a will of their own?[10]

---

[9] Mary Wollstonecraft, *A Vindication of the Rights of Woman* (Dublin, 1793), 4.

[10] Charles Francis Adams, *The Works of John Adams, Second President Of The United States: With A Life Of The Author, Notes And Illustrations*, vol. IX (Little, Brown and Company, 1854), 373–76.

Ownership of property determined the right to vote, from which women were unquestionably excluded. Most women complacently accepted their status of domesticity, hardly considering another option while weathering waves of economic poverty and social hardships. But a small faction of women refused to accept the injustice of their voiceless dependence on men in society.

The American suffrage movement began to gather strength in the mid-nineteenth century, revolting against the exclusion of women from education, marital and property rights, and the right to vote. These women did not want their fate to continue to rest upon the character and decisions of others. Susan B. Anthony soberly wrote about women in unequal social structures: "Compelled by their position in society to depend on men for subsistence, for food, clothes, shelter, for every chance even to earn a dollar, they have no way of escape from the besotted victims of appetite and passion with whom their lot is cast."[11]

Although many strands of women's activism are woven throughout different ages and cultures, the nineteenth century was a time of great political change for women. Decades of relentless advocacy and thousands of women's efforts came to fruition in the ratification of the Nineteenth Amendment to the US Constitution on August 18, 1920, which guaranteed all American women the right to vote. As is often the case, the activists best known for agitating to bring the amendment to pass didn't live to see its enactment.

---

[11]   Harper, *The Life and Work of Susan B. Anthony*, vol. II, 1004.

Fighting Her Disenfranchisement – Nineteenth Century

"Women, and mothers in particular, should feel it their right and duty to extend their influence beyond the circumference of the home circle, and to say what circumstances shall surround children when they go forth from under the watchful guardianship of the mother's love; for certain it is that, if the customs and laws of society remain corrupt as they now are, the best and wisest of the mother's teachings will soon be counteracted."[12]

—Susan B. Anthony, 1852

From among the many women who faithfully contributed to the nineteenth-century woman's movement emerged an unlikely pair: Susan B. Anthony and Elizabeth Cady Stanton, whose fifty-year friendship changed the course of American history. Still today, two hundred years later, Susan B. Anthony, the Quaker woman born in 1820 Massachusetts, is a threat. Her legacy incites racial battles and feminist disputes, just as her name and reputation had during her lifetime. We still struggle with the movement's mouthpiece being a well-to-do white woman from a comfortable

---

[12]   Harper, *The Life and Work of Susan B. Anthony*, vol. I, 71.

upbringing who enjoyed relative equality under the Quaker law. She refused to stay quietly on the fringes of society with the other single women of her time. Instead, Susan became a radical; relentlessly seeking a better place for women in the family, community, church body, and according to the law.

Elizabeth Cady Stanton is another fascinating key figure in the women's rights movement, particularly because while Susan B. Anthony remained single and fully devoted to her public mission, Elizabeth was equally impactful while at the same time remaining a faithful wife and mother to seven children. Elizabeth inspired leading abolitionist and women's rights activist Lucretia Mott, among other active Quaker women, to organize the first Women's Rights Convention in 1848. Despite its organizers enduring harsh criticism and public disgrace, the metaphorical ball was set in motion at that Seneca Falls convention, which has since marked the start of an organized women's movement in the United States.

With an iron will and backbone of steel, no activist was dearer to Susan B. Anthony than the well-known Elizabeth Cady Stanton. The extraordinary strength of their fifty-year friendship was formed as much by their own passions as by the humility of each to recognize her weaknesses and the strengths of her friend. Out of this, their almost comical friendship developed over years of Susan wrangling Elizabeth's unruly brood of children while encouraging Elizabeth to write, and in turn, Elizabeth accompanying and supporting her rabble-rousing friend in all of her brazen endeavors. Elizabeth recalled, "It was 'mid such exhilarating scenes [such as a neighbor rescuing her eighteen-month-old from the highest peak of the chimney where he was put by his older brother and her five-year-old skinning his hands sliding down the lightning rod] that Miss Anthony and I wrote addresses for temperance, anti-slavery, educational, and woman's rights conventions."[13]

The two met at an anti-slavery meeting in Seneca Falls, solidifying their friendship by working exuberantly together to establish a co-educational college, which became the precursor to Cornell University, the first co-ed Ivy League university. They continued to successfully work together, forming the Woman's State Temperance Convention. Elizabeth crafted the thunderbolts and Susan fired them from the "domestic watchtower" of Elizabeth's home as the two "forged resolutions, protests, appeals, petitions, . . . and constitutional arguments." Elizabeth wrote in her autobiography that together the duo relentlessly challenged "false interpretations of Bible texts, the statistics of women robbed of their property, shut out of some college, half paid for their work, the reports of some disgraceful trial; injustice enough to turn any woman's thoughts from stockings and puddings."[14] Their friendship became a legacy built upon deep respect, stimulating companionship, sharing Elizabeth's domestic cares, and the insatiable need to address injustice.

The constant conventions, speeches, and letters in newspapers formed by the army of women siding with Susan B. Anthony and Elizabeth Cady Stanton not only challenged

---

[13]   Elizabeth Cady Stanton, *Eighty Years and More: Reminiscences 1815–1897* (New York: European Publishing Company, 1898), 164.

[14]   Ibid., 165.

the Constitution of this country but also asked the existential question of who women are—both in the eyes of God and in the eyes of men. For the first time, the questions of justice, human freedom, republicanism, and civil and social rights were being publicly pondered by women. Women began challenging their exclusive confinement to the private sphere, and men also soon found it impossible not to consider their very capable and wise mothers, teachers, wives, sisters, and daughters who were being unjustly forsaken and abandoned by the law.

Susan's dedication to the cause amazed Elizabeth, who saw Susan as a passionate mother of ideas rather than of men. Susan instantly recognized Elizabeth's great talent and skill for writing and encouraged her to continue writing speeches and publishing articles, voluntarily watching Elizabeth's spirited children as she hid away in her office writing. And so, in the midst of rebellious children locking each other in the smoke-house, shooting themselves in the hand with a pistol, and experimenting on the baby with a life preserver made of corks thrown into the cold river, Elizabeth was able to write newspaper articles and speeches and accept speaking engagements. Elizabeth said of Susan in her autobiography, "With the cares of a large family I might, in time, like too many women, have become wholly absorbed in a narrow family selfishness, had not my friend been continually exploring new fields for missionary labors."[15]

Elizabeth struggled; remaining strongly devoted to her family while persistently being called to greater participation

---

[15]   Ibid.

in the cause. She clarified her divided allegiance between work and family in a letter to Susan dated 1853, "My whole soul is in the work, but my hands belong to my family." In choosing to bridge the gap between motherhood and public affairs, Elizabeth hardly ever escaped the criticism that shadowed her. In her time, the most persistent objection against women entering politics was the inevitable cause to neglect their home and family. Susan B. Anthony, though not a physical mother, refuted this argument in 1902 with a storehouse of inspirational wisdom:

> Women do not love their families because compelled to do so by statute, or cling to their homes because there is no place for them outside . . . although the entire status of women has been changed, and they are largely engaged in the public work of every community, they are better and happier wives, mothers and housekeepers because they are more intelligent and live a broader life. But they are learning, and the world is learning, that their housekeeping qualities should extend to the municipality and their power of motherhood to the children of the whole nation, and that these should be expressed through this very politics from which they are so rigorously excluded.[16]

Rather than divide a woman between the public and private sphere, demanding that she choose either her motherhood or participation in public life, such as voting, Susan

---

[16]   Susan B. Anthony, *History of Woman Suffrage*, vol. IV. (New York: 1902), xxxi.

realized that each aspect strengthened the other. She began an early secular debate that was later theologically elevated by St. John Paul II, who said that a woman "discovers herself through a sincere gift of self."[17] This free and fruitful gift of self is necessary in the home as well as in society. The vocation of a wife and mother is ultimately born of love rather than of an obligation or lack of other opportunity. Susan recognized that when these vocations are cherished and protected, and when women are also granted participation in their government, all spheres will benefit from her maternal qualities.

The Revolution Newspaper (1868–1872)

The nineteenth century could easily be called a war of morality through the press. Newspapers began cropping up to disseminate free thought and explore new radical ideas of government and society. Likewise, ads for abortion, contraception, and "quack" medicines littered back pages and columns of newspapers whose editors struggled between morality and financial survival. Congress's passage of the Comstock Act in 1873, which prohibited advertising, distributing, and the use of birth control, forced publishers who would otherwise promote such "obscene content" to reconsider publication or be more discreet in its distribution. But there are always those who will defy a law when their financial interests depend on it, and so pornography, contraceptive powders, devices, and manuals on birth

---

[17]   John Paul II, On the Dignity and Vocation of Women *Mulieris Dignitatem* (August 15, 1988), no. 6.

control were discreetly passed under bookstore counters, basement offices, and mailed in unlabeled envelopes. As nineteenth-century author Joseph Hertford observed, "The public press can exert a most powerful influence either for good or for evil," advancing civilization or degrading it so low "by creating a morbid appetite for such novelties as neither tend to elevate the mind nor the heart."[18]

The country was in need of elevation. It was 1868, three years since slavery had been abolished and still two years away from black men gaining the right to vote. Women would have to wait another long fifty-two years until they could cast their ballots. Yet this significant year for American women saw two pioneers—Susan B. Anthony and Elizabeth Cady Stanton—launch the first weekly women's newspaper.

Serving as the official voice of the National Woman Suffrage Association, the newspaper "created a sensation such as scarcely ever has been equalled by any publication,"[19] wrote fellow suffragette and author of Susan B. Anthony's three-volume biography, Ida Husted Harper, in 1898. While many well-known newspapers and politicians of the day published attacks and critical reviews of *The Revolution*, the suffragettes' publication gained high-profile subscribers, including President Andrew Johnson.

Despite the paper's short life, Susan and Elizabeth succeeded at provoking social thought and publicly challenging many cases of disenfranchisement, all while refusing to accept advertisements for morally evil products and

---

[18]   Joseph Hertford, *Personals: Or, Perils of the Period, Printed for the Author* (New York, 1870), 7.

[19]   Harper, *The Life and Work of Susan B. Anthony*, vol. I, 295.

procedures, such as abortion. Elizabeth somberly reflected on *The Revolution*'s plight after her four years as the paper's editor, "So long as the public will pay for gross personalities, obscenity, and slang, decent journals will be outbidden in the market."[20]

The Revolution, as it was fittingly named, was said by *The New York Sunday Times* under a section titled *The Ladies Militant* to be "charged to the muzzle with literary nitre-glycerine." It stirred those who had grown apathetic after the Civil War back into the fight for women's rights. The paper's controversial positions challenged social norms, marital dynamics, spousal obedience, women's fashion, voting, and even taboo topics like domestic violence. But not all enemies of *The Revolution* were from the opposing side. Fellow abolitionists and suffragettes from the American Equal Rights Association believed the paper would antagonize Republicans and divert the primary focus from black suffrage.

Finding it insulting that injustice couldn't be fought on several fronts at the same time, Elizabeth dismissed the various attacks as "the united effort of Republicans, Abolitionists and certain women to crush us and our paper."[21] Those crushing blows actively increased, however, as she challenged woman's rights in marriage. She recalled in her autobiography, "So many things, that I had neither thought nor said, were attributed to me that, at times, I really doubted my own identity."[22]

---

[20] Stanton, *Eighty Years and More,* 275.
[21] Harper, *The Life and Work of Susan B. Anthony,* vol. I, 300.
[22] Stanton, *Eighty Years and More,* 225.

Abolitionists and suffragettes continued to clash in regards to the prioritization of suffrage. The consensus among several prominent abolitionists, including Frederick Douglass, held that each generation was prepared to accept only one new change—the first being "negro suffrage." Many were afraid to split focus due to the progress which had already been made in that area, coupled with the tenable fear of facing another Civil War. Several abolitionists vocally called the suffragettes to stand down for the next few generations, on the basis that there was no fear of women avenging themselves. *The Revolution* recalled their harrowing words: "One idea for a generation, to come up in the order of their importance. First negro suffrage, then temperance, then the eight-hour movement, then woman suffrage. Three generations hence, woman suffrage will be in order! . . . This is the time to settle the rights of races; unless we do justice to the negro we shall bring down on ourselves another bloody revolution, another four years' war, but we have nothing to fear from woman, she will not avenge herself!"[23]

Susan and Elizabeth never halted from unleashing their full fury through the columns of *The Revolution,* responding, "Woman not avenge herself? Look at your asylums for the deaf, the dumb, the blind, the insane, and there behold the results of this wholesale desecration of the mothers of the race! Woman not avenge herself? Go into the streets of your cities at the midnight hour, and there behold those whom God meant to be queens in the moral universe giving your sons their first lessons in infamy and vice. No, you can not

---

[23]   Harper, *The Life and Work of Susan B. Anthony,* vol. I, 300–1.

Anthonys continued to assist with rendezvous houses for runaway slaves.

Although Susan spiritually strayed from the Quaker church and embraced Unitarianism and ultimately an agnostic outlook, which focused on social work over religious beliefs, she was accustomed to women holding high positions in the Quaker churches and discussing business and politics in mixed company. This didn't prepare her well for being silenced at teachers' conventions and in the public sphere. In 1852, after fifteen years of teaching, Susan left the classroom to dedicate all her efforts publicly toward temperance, anti-slavery, and eventually women's rights. Her parents and sister Mary attended the first Women's Rights Convention in Seneca Falls, held by Elizabeth Cady Stanton and Lucrecia Mott in 1848, each signing the declaration for equal rights for women.

Throughout her long public career, Susan stoically waded through many arguments crafted to deny women the right to vote: mental incapacity, business incompetency, bondage of tradition, prejudice, creed, politics, progress of public sentiment, legislative enfranchisement, taxation, and what she called the most persistent objection of all: the fear that women's entrance into politics would inevitably cause them to neglect their home and family.

Dedicating over fifty years of her life to gain rights for the disenfranchised, Susan B. Anthony led the women's rights movement. She spoke at conventions, published articles, and canvassed door-to-door across the country. Upon her death on March 13, 1906, the *Evening Times* reported, "Women well may mourn. The soul of a system and a creed left the world last night when Susan B. Anthony crossed the Great Divide. The dominant mind that guided the destinies of the greatest women's movement of the century is stilled. A soul, the greatness of which it remains for posterity to discover, shook off its fettering clay and soared to its place in the empyrean. Women well may mourn."[30]

Elizabeth Cady Stanton Wanted It All

In 1868, the *New York Sunday Times* wrote, "If Mrs. Stanton would attend a little more to her domestic duties and a little less to those of the great public, perhaps she would exalt her sex quite as much as she does by Quixotically fighting windmills in their gratuitous behalf, and she might possibly set a notable example of domestic felicity. No married woman can convert herself into a feminine Knight of the Rueful Visage and ride about the country attempting to redress imaginary wrongs without leaving her own household in a neglected condition that must be an eloquent witness against her."[31]

But even in her day, Elizabeth Cady Stanton refused to abandon either her family or the fight for women's rights. As the daughter of a New York state lawyer, judge, and congressman, she possessed a strong counter-cultural desire to participate in government from an early age. She absorbed a legal education through the countless hours she spent in her father's busy home office. Recognizing the great legal disparity of women and black people according to the law, Elizabeth lacked no courage in outwardly challenging either.

---

[30]   Harper, *The Life and Work of Susan B. Anthony*, vol. III, 1425.
[31]   Harper, *The Life and Work of Susan B. Anthony*, vol. I, 295–96.

From an early age, Elizabeth Cady struggled to reconcile her own self-worth with society's devaluing of women.
She remembered vividly "that girls were considered an infe-
rior order of beings," and when her little sister was born,
she overheard many visiting friends remark, "What a pity
it is she's a girl!"[32] One treasured son and five daughters in
the Cady family survived past infancy. But when Elizabeth
was only eleven years old, devastation struck as her twen-
ty-year-old brother, in whom all future hopes and dreams
were invested, died unexpectedly. It was in that catastrophic
moment that Elizabeth's future took shape, forming her purpose and ambition in life. Witnessing the torrent of despair
consuming her poor father, Elizabeth desperately tried to
console him with her presence. "Oh, my daughter, I wish
you were a boy!" he responded. Elizabeth replied with stead-
fast conviction, "I will try to be all my brother was."[33]

Remaining true to that promise for the rest of her life,
Elizabeth became relentlessly determined to master her two
perceived elements of masculinity: education and courage.
Possessing these would make her as much like a boy as she
thought possible. She immediately began studying Greek,
learned to manage a horse, and pushed herself to meet every
physical limit. But despite her immense progress and ardent
efforts to impress her father, he was never convinced that she
was as good as a boy. Crushed and more determined than
ever to prove herself to him, Elizabeth studied Latin, Greek,
and mathematics with a class of boys. Surpassing them all

---

[32]   Stanton, *Eighty Years and More*, 4.
[33]   Ibid., 21.

and winning first prize in Greek, Elizabeth rushed to her father for validation. Again, and to her detriment, he simply concluded, "Ah, you should have been a boy!"[34]

Elizabeth experienced further disappointment when the one man, Rev. Simon Hosack, whom she loved as a father and who praised and guided her early pursuits died. She devoted her time thereafter in her father's law office, absorbed in women's complaints of unjust laws restraining their personal property, rights to their children, and their lack of social freedom. Between her father's tireless explanations of the existing laws concerning women and the cold incessant teasing by his law students on the depraved state of American women, Elizabeth became hell-bent on changing those laws by any means possible.

She soon faced insult to injury, being left behind by her college-bound male classmates, despite being at the top of her class at graduation. Despising the great chasm of her sex, Elizabeth wrote, "It seemed to me that every book taught the 'divinely ordained' headship of man, but my mind never yielded to this popular heresy."[35]

Reluctantly attending Mrs. Willard's Seminary at Troy, a fashionable school for girls, in 1830, Elizabeth solidified her conviction "that it is a grave mistake to send boys and girls to separate institutions of learning, especially at the most impressionable age."[36] As soon as she returned home from the seminary, Elizabeth studied analysis and logic from her brother-in-law. She also discovered a new zeal in debating

---

[34]   Ibid., 23.
[35]   Ibid., 34.
[36]   Ibid., 37.

with her father's conceited law students who had recently graduated from college, particularly about woman's equality. Elizabeth wrote in her autobiography, "I confess that I did not study so much for love of the truth or my own development, in these days, as to make those young men recognize my equality."[37]

In her young adulthood, Elizabeth spent several weeks of the year at the home of their wealthy and well-known relative: the abolitionist Gerrit Smith of Peterboro, NY. Years of gathering at Smith's lively residence influenced Elizabeth to shed her Calvinistic fears of inescapable damnation, replacing them with actionable humanitarian concerns over slavery, temperance, and individual rights. Smith, whose mansion was one of the stations on the underground railroad, not only devoted his personal wealth towards these abolitionist activities but also assumed social and personal risk by aiding escaped slaves to reach freedom.

It is Gerrit Smith who led Elizabeth furtively to a room on his third floor one evening in 1839 where she met an escaped slave for the first time. Harriet Powel, a beautiful young woman labeled at the time a "quadroon" (meaning one quarter African heritage). Harriet recounted the haunting history of her enslavement to Elizabeth for the next few hours and the unwelcome attention and heartbreak her beauty had wrought upon her since adolescence. Elizabeth wept bitterly during this encounter and said she and her cousins "needed no further education to make us earnest abolitionists." Elizabeth also took the opportunity to ask

---

[37]   Ibid., 48.

Harriet about the parallel laws between women and slaves. As recorded in an authoritative source compiled by the suffragettes themselves, Harriet soberly responded, "Yes, but I am both. I am doubly damned in sex and color. Yea, in class too, for I am poor and ignorant; none of you can ever touch the depth of misery where I stand to-day."[38]

As Harriet Powel made the dangerous journey from Smith's house to Canada, Elizabeth's cousin Gerrit delayed Harriet's slave owner until news confirmed her safe Canadian arrival. Harriet became famously known as the "fair fugitive," and Smith published an open letter to her slave owner in the *New York Tribune* in 1839. Harriet is but one of the dozens of slaves Gerrit Smith helped to reach freedom, and his estate now houses the National Abolition Hall of Fame. The *New York Times* wrote on December 29, 1874, "The history of the most important half century of our national life will be imperfectly written if it fails to place Gerrit Smith in the front rank of the men whose influence was most felt in the accomplishment of its results."[39]

Meeting Harriet at Peterboro was Elizabeth's greatest education on slavery and her gateway into abolitionism. Like Susan, Elizabeth prioritized rational ideas and scientific facts over religion. She admired both religious reformers and agnostics alike who focused more on the good that could be done in this world rather than what she considered to be agonizing over the unknowns of the next. Coming to this personal spiritual awakening profoundly resonated with

---

[38]   *VOTES FOR WOMEN*, 406.
[39]   *NY Times*, vol. XXIV, no. 7265, December 29, 1874.

her throughout the rest of her life. She reflected on it in her autobiography, saying, "The old bondage of fear of the visible and the invisible was broken and, no longer subject to absolute authority, I rejoiced in the dawn of a new day of freedom in thought and action."[40] This "freedom" from absolute authority, however, would continue to trouble Elizabeth and contribute to her interpreting her own blasphemous version of the Bible.

But Peterboro held one more treasure for Elizabeth. Elizabeth first heard at Peterboro "the most eloquent and impassioned orator on the anti-slavery platform, Henry B. Stanton."[41] She was drawn to Henry, who was ten years older than her, through his strength of character and contagious passion for abolitionism. Elizabeth and Henry began spending their leisure time together. But despite her growing attraction to Henry, the constant discussions with peers over unjust laws regarding women in the married state, and objections from her family and friends over marrying an outspoken abolitionist, caused Elizabeth to end the engagement. She renewed it again after months of anxiety, and Elizabeth and Henry were married on May 11, 1840—on the condition that the word "obey" was removed from their ceremonial vows. Elizabeth stated, "I obstinately refused to obey one with whom I supposed I was entering into an equal relationship."[42]

Newly married to a progressive delegate, Elizabeth travelled with Henry to England for the World's Anti-Slavery

---

40   Stanton, *Eighty Years and More*, 45.
41   Ibid., 58.
42   Ibid., 72.

Convention. There she became uncomfortably aware of the split within the movement, dividing the political abolitionists of Henry's party from the Garrisonian branch. Named after abolitionist and women's rights advocate William Lloyd Garrison, their members supported women speaking and voting at conventions. The Garrisonians were overruled and the female delegates were rejected from participating at the convention. Elizabeth was appalled, writing, "It struck me as very remarkable that abolitionists, who felt so keenly the wrongs of the slave, should be so oblivious to the equal wrongs of their own mothers, wives, and sisters, when, according to the common law, both classes occupied a similar legal status."[43] After spending a considerable amount of time overseas with Lucretia Mott, one of the rejected female American delegates at the convention, both were inspired to return to America with new vigor in the fight for women's rights.

At first, Elizabeth took an active part in New York legislation, between the births of her children, championing the Married Women's Property bill. But, contrary to her previous judgment of downtrodden mothers sulking in disordered households, Elizabeth began to understand. Home life in Seneca Falls was increasingly overwhelming and none of her numerous duties challenged her higher faculties. She suffered from "mental hunger" and a lack of stimulating companionship that gave way to depression. When her household was struck with malaria, Elizabeth concluded, "Cleanliness, order, the love of the beautiful and artistic, all faded away

---

43   Ibid., 79.

in the struggle to accomplish what was absolutely necessary from hour to hour. . . . The general discontent I felt with woman's portion as wife, mother, housekeeper, physician, and spiritual guide, the chaotic conditions into which everything fell without her constant supervision, and the wearied, anxious look of the majority of women impressed me with a strong feeling that some active measures should be taken to remedy the wrongs of society in general, and of women in particular."[44]

Taxation Without Representation

Susan and Elizabeth had significantly more freedom than most women of their time, due to Susan's single state and Elizabeth's supportive husband. As an unmarried woman, Susan could even make and sign legal documents, own and dispose of property, and control her own wages. But Susan and Elizabeth were activated by the awareness that women's painful limitations in the country extended beyond their own.

Laws concerning married women hadn't advanced much since they were penned by the English eighteenth-century justice Sir William Blackstone. Blackstone's *Commentaries on the Laws of England* strongly influenced the development of the American legal system and was largely responsible for the depersonalizing language of married women according to the law. The worst of the commentaries followed a principle of coverture, stating that all prior rights of a woman were absorbed by her husband at the time of marriage: "By

---

[44]   Ibid., 147–48.

marriage, the husband and wife are one person in law: that is, the very being or legal existence of the woman is suspended during the marriage, or at least is incorporated and consolidated into that of the husband."[45]

Elizabeth summed up Blackstone's coverture commentary as "the husband and wife are one, and that one is the husband," in a letter to the editor of the *New York Tribune* in 1861.[46] Our American government unquestionably adopted the British concept of coverture, which seemingly contradicted their grievance of "taxation without representation." Even Abigail Adams noted this when she wrote to her husband John on March 31, 1776: "And, by the way, in the new code of laws which I suppose it will be necessary for you to make, I desire you would remember the ladies and be more generous and favorable to them than your ancestors. Do not put such unlimited power into the hands of the husbands. . . . If particular care and attention is not paid to the ladies, we are determined to foment a rebellion, and will not hold ourselves bound by any laws in which we have no voice or representation."[47]

According to Blackstone, woman ceased to legally exist when the two became one flesh in marriage. As an extension of her husband, she could not own property, earn money, make contracts, or have legal guardianship of her children

---

[45]   William Blackstone, *Commentaries on the Laws of England, Book I: Of the Rights of Persons* (Oxford: Clarendon Press, 1765), 430.

[46]   Stanton, *Eighty Years and More*, 221.

[47]   Charles Francis Adams, "Braintree by Abigail Adams - 31 March, 1776," *Familiar Letters of John Adams and his Wife Abigail Adams during the Revolution* (New York: Hurd and Houghton, 1876), 149–50.

without his consent. A deceased wife was the relict or rem-
nant of her husband. This misguided understanding of the
scriptural union of one flesh grossly distorted the sacred
covenant of marriage. Many women entering marriage as a
means of survival discovered Blackstone's coverture to be a
source of enmity. It should come as no surprise that Susan B.
Anthony advised women, as was recorded in a letter in 1859,
"take to her soul a strong purpose and that on her tombstone
shall be engraved her own name and her own noble deeds
instead of merely . . . the relict of some Honorable."[48]

The concept of coverture provoked many problems, especially in cases of alcoholic and abusive husbands. Elizabeth
regularly encountered this detriment when assisting women
in the neighboring Irish community that she had befriended.
Tired of watching helpless mothers bear the financial ruin of
alcoholic and reckless husbands, Elizabeth delivered a powerful speech to five hundred women at a Rochester convention in 1852, saying, "Let us petition our State government
so to modify the laws affecting marriage and the custody of
children, that the drunkard shall have no claims on wife or
child."[49]

When Susan and fellow suffragette Amelia Bloomer
appeared as welcomed delegates at the *Men's State Temperance Convention*, they were publicly shamed by a reverend
from Albany, who called the two "a hybrid species, half man
and half woman, belonging to neither sex."[50] This attack on
their femininity proved to be a regular weapon used against

---

[48]   Harper, *The Life and Work of Susan B. Anthony*, vol. I, 183.
[49]   Ibid., 67.
[50]   Ibid., 69–70.

the suffragettes. It neither deterred nor caused Elizabeth and Susan to question themselves as women.

Susan was made secretary of the Woman's Rights Convention in Syracuse on September 8, 1852, under president Lucretia Mott. Although religion and the Bible were continuously used against the women's movement, the suffragettes gained the support of many men and Christian leaders taking up the cause. Unitarian minister Amory Dwight Mayo wrote in support of the 1852 Convention: "The assertion that woman is responsible to man for her belief or conduct, in any other sense than man is responsible to woman, I reject, not as a believer in any theory of 'woman's rights,' but as a believer in that religion which knows neither male nor female in its imperative demand upon the individual conscience."[51]

Still, the excessive misuse of Scripture as a weapon caused many involved, including Elizabeth, to cast doubts on the Bible's definitive authority. Americans feared renouncing the concept of coverture. What would happen to the family if women had the freedom to divorce, gain custody, and control their own finances? Ernestine L. Rose, a Jewish escapee from Poland, whom suffragette Ida Husted Harper called "the queen of the platform," courageously addressed the Convention crowd:

> We ask for our rights not as a gift of charity, but as an act of justice; for it is in accordance with the principles of republicanism that, as woman has to pay taxes to maintain government, she has a right to participate

---

[51]   Ibid., 73.

in the formation and administration of it; that as she is amenable to the laws of her country, she is entitled to a voice in their enactment and to all the protective advantages they can bestow; that as she is as liable as man to all the vicissitudes of life, she ought to enjoy the same social rights and privileges. Any difference, therefore, in political, civil and social rights, on account of sex, is in direct violation of the principles of justice and humanity, and as such ought to be held up to the contempt and derision of every lover of human freedom.[52]

Susan B. Anthony said that the ballot was the symbol of power in a republic, stating in a speech given in 1875, "Hence, our first and most urgent demand—that women shall be protected in the exercise of their inherent, personal, citizen's right to a voice in the government, municipal, state, national."[53] The suffragettes fought for the inalienable rights of all Americans to be recognized according to the laws of the United States Constitution. They reminded the country that the denial of the female minority[54] to participate in government echoed the divine authority of kings that America had revolted against.

---

[52]   *VOTES FOR WOMEN,* 5228.

[53]   Harper, *The Life and Work of Susan B. Anthony,* vol. II, 1007.

[54]   There were four million full- or part-time working women over age twenty-one in 1875.

The Ballot and the Bullet

When Susan attended the New York Constitutional Convention in 1867, she was directly challenged by future presidential nominee Horace Greeley on the *ballot and the bullet* argument against women's enfranchisement. Greeley asked, "Miss Anthony, you know the ballot and the bullet go together. If you vote, are you ready to fight?" Susan responded, "Yes, Mr. Greeley, just as you fought in the late war—at the point of a goose-quill! . . . My right as a human being is as good as that of any other human being. If you have a right to vote at twenty-one, then I have. All we ask is that you shall take down the bars and let the women and the negroes in, then we will settle all these matters."[55]

The irony of justice did not elude the suffragettes. Disenfranchised black soldiers and slaves had unofficially fought in the Revolutionary War, the War of 1812, and at the start of the Civil War in 1861. When Abraham Lincoln issued the Emancipation Proclamation in 1863, black men were accepted for the first time into the Union Army and Navy, allowing the liberated to become liberators. Fredrick Douglass believed that the enlistment of black men would reclaim black manhood, advocating, "You owe it to yourself and your race to rise from your social debasement and take your place among the soldiers of your country, a man among men. . . . Thus in defending your country now against rebels and traitors you are defending your own liberty, honor, manhood, and self-respect."[56] Slavery was abolished two years later, in

[55]   Harper, *The Life and Work of Susan B. Anthony*, vol. I, 278.

[56]   Nicholas Buccola, *The Essential Douglass: Selected Writings and*

1865, with the ratification of the Thirteenth Amendment. Black men were granted the right to vote five years later, with the ratification of the Fifteenth Amendment. For black men, the ballot and the bullet didn't always go together, but by 1870, they had both. It was still another fifty years until women were granted the same right to vote.

Susan and Elizabeth firmly believed that the military argument lacked substantial value, claiming that wives and mothers had equally sacrificed their loved ones for the sake of liberty. Elizabeth reflected on women's efforts in the outbreak of the Civil War in 1861: "The labor women accomplished, the hardships they endured, the time and strength they sacrificed in the War that summoned three million men to arms, can never be fully appreciated."[57]

Writing in the introduction of Volume IV of *The History of Woman Suffrage* in 1900, Susan recalled that the military argument had lost its power, saying, "It would also disfranschise [sic] vast numbers of men; that the value of women in the perpetuation of the Government is at least equal to that of the men who defend it; and that there is no recognition in the laws by which the franchise is exercised of the slightest connection between a ballot and a bullet."[58]

Speeches (Indianapolis: Hackett Publishing Company, Inc., 2016), 189.
[57]   Stanton, *Eighty Years and More*, 234–35.
[58]   Anthony, *History of Woman Suffrage*, xxxi.

The Brave Old Maid and
the Feminine Knight

As she prepared her first address to the New York legislature in February 1854, Elizabeth once again faced a former demon: the unwinnable opinion of her father. Fearing his disapproval but honoring his request, she passionately read her speech to him alone in his office one night. After a long silence at her conclusion, she noticed tears in his eyes, indicative of how her words had moved him. His silence gave way to confusion that a woman of such comfortable upbringing could so intimately understand the unexperienced wrongs of her sex. Surrounded by the familiar legal books and comfort of her father's office, Elizabeth explained to him that it was there. Amid years of studying unjust laws and overhearing female clients' misery, her deepest sympathies toward suffrage had grown into an unquenchable passion.

Susan printed twenty thousand copies of Elizabeth's speech and distributed them to every member of legislature throughout the state. The critics attacked immediately and mercilessly, steering public opinion. The *Albany Register* released an article on March 7, 1854, asking "how far public sentiment should sanction or tolerate these unsexed women, who would step out from the true sphere of the mother, the wife, and the daughter, and taking upon themselves the duties and the business of men, stalk into the public gaze."[59] Men supporting the suffrage platform were so shamefully embarrassed in print, as was also demonstrated in the *Albany Register* article, that many backed down to save their reputation and career: "Such men there are always, and, honest or dishonest, their true position is that of being tied to the apron strings of some strong-minded woman, and to be exhibited as rare specimens of human wickedness or human weakness and folly."[60]

As mother of a large family, and in the public eye, Elizabeth faced the contempt of men hailing from legislative offices and from behind the printed words of newspapers. Moreover, she detested responding to the deprecating women who inquired on the whereabouts of her children during her public lectures. Elizabeth recalled an instance after her legislative address, in which she exercised her memorable sharp wit: "Ladies, it takes me no longer to speak, than you to listen; what have you done with your children the two hours you have been sitting here?"[61] Likewise, when fashionable women objected to the publicity and immodesty of the women's rights movement, Elizabeth was quick to call their bluff as well:

> Really, ladies, you surprise me; our conventions are not
> as public as the ballroom where I saw you all dancing

---

[59]   Stanton, *Eighty Years and More*, 190–91.
[60]   Ibid.
[61]   Ibid., 192.

last night. As to modesty, it may be a question, in many minds, whether it is less modest to speak words of soberness and truth, plainly dressed on a platform, than gorgeously arrayed, with bare arms and shoulders, to waltz in the arms of strange gentlemen. And as to the press, I noticed you all reading, in this morning's papers, with evident satisfaction, the personal compliments and full descriptions of your dresses at the last ball. . . . When my name is mentioned, it is in connection with some great reform movement.[62]

Very few pioneers of reform—such as Elizabeth and Susan— find their cause worthy enough to continually endure the risk and overcome their discomfort and self-preserving pride. As William H. Seward, secretary of state under Abraham Lincoln, confessed to Elizabeth at a dinner party, "You have the argument, but custom and prejudice are against you, and they are stronger than truth and logic."[63]

This was evident in the "dark secrets of insane asylums," which Elizabeth recalled discovering in the winter of 1861. She and Susan helped an abused mother of one of New York's first families escape with her child, after being unjustly "incarcerated in an insane asylum for eighteen months."[64] Elizabeth was horrified to learn of the similar confinement of many other women, due to inconvenience or their rebellion against their husband. She wrote in her autobiography, "We should be shocked to know the great number of rebellious

---

[62]   Ibid., 196.
[63]   Ibid., 199.
[64]   Ibid., 213.

wives, sisters, and daughters who are thus sacrificed to false customs and barbarous laws made by men for women." To Susan and Elizabeth it was "as imperative a duty to shield a sane mother, who had been torn from a family of little children and doomed to the companionship of lunatics, and to aid her in fleeing to a place of safety, as to help a fugitive from slavery to Canada."[65]

Elizabeth aroused further speculation as one of the only women speaking on the subject of divorce at the time. She was inspired by radical socialist reformer and former Indiana representative Robert Dale Owen, whose divorce legislation was publicly criticized by abolitionist Horace Greeley, who said, "The lax principles of Robert Dale Owen . . . combined to establish, some years since, a state of law which enables men or women to get unmarried nearly at pleasure."[66] When Lucrecia, Elizabeth, and Susan added the reconstruction of the marriage system to their platform at the National Woman's Rights Convention in 1861, the decision was criticized even among friends. Elizabeth recalled thirty-seven years later in her autobiography, "The trouble was not in what I said, but that I said it too soon, and before the people were ready to hear it."[67]

Elizabeth called for marriage to be defined and understood as a loving companionship between a man and woman and that children be soberly educated on its sacredness and responsibilities: "The first step toward making the ideal the

---

[65]   Ibid., 214.

[66]   Horace Greeley, *Recollections of a Busy Life* (New York: J.B. Ford and Company, 1868), 571.

[67]   Stanton, *Eighty Years and More*, 216.

real, is to educate our sons and daughters into the most exalted ideas of the sacredness of married life and the responsibilities of parenthood. I would have them give, at least, as much thought to the creation of an immortal being as the artist gives to his landscape or statue. . . . To this impressionable period of human life . . . we must begin to cultivate virtues that can alone redeem the world."[68]

That winter of 1861, following the election of Lincoln, Elizabeth and Susan became the target of mobs while on a series of anti-slavery conventions in the Northern cities. Elizabeth and other suffragettes had also renounced the restrictive fashion of the customary female garments and embraced the "bloomer," which Elizabeth recalled being "like a captive set free from his ball and chain, I was always ready for a brisk walk through sleet and snow and rain, to climb a mountain, jump over a fence, work in the garden, and, in fact, for any necessary locomotion."[69] But public scorn was so merciless toward them that even Elizabeth toned down her convenient wardrobe for the sake of her acquaintances and friends.

These setbacks didn't stop her from launching a twelve-year speaking career at the end of 1869, lecturing steadily from Maine to Texas for eight months of every year. She slept in a rat-infested bed while canvasing the pioneer state of Kansas and bore fifty-mile sleigh rides through Northern Iowa . Each state had to be won by the suffragettes independently. Wyoming, for example, allowed women to vote as early as 1869. Mormon women in Salt Lake City, who

---

[68]   Ibid., 230.
[69]   Ibid., 201.

Elizabeth recalled considered voting "as much a duty as to say her prayers,"[70] gained the vote a year later in 1870.

But meeting Ohio representative John Bingham on the California leg of her lecture tour was most memorable for Elizabeth. Despite telling her that "he was not the puppet of logic, but the slave of practical politics," Bingham went on to author the first section of the Fourteenth Amendment, using universal language in framing its Equal Protection Clause. Susan attempted to use Bingham's clause when she illegally cast her vote in the 1872 election in Rochester, New York. She and other women were jailed for voting until pardoned by President Ulysses S. Grant.

Then, in the centennial year of 1876, the suffragettes dedicated the Fourth of July as a "woman's day," to be celebrated with speeches and the reading of their *own* declaration of rights. Susan B. Anthony and four other suffragettes were among the few women granted entrance into the public celebration in Philadelphia for the reading of the Declaration of 1776. Directly following its reading by founding father Richard Henry Lee, Susan quickly made her way to the platform, defying the prohibition to read her declaration publicly. In front of Independence Hall, in the shadow of the liberty bell, Susan read the Woman's Declaration of Rights.

Faith and Suffrage

In the wake of the death of Lucrecia Mott, the monumental activist, on November 11, 1880, Elizabeth and Susan, along with Matilda Joslyn Gage and Ida Husted Harper, wrote the

---

[70]   Ibid., 287.

History of Woman Suffrage. It was published in six volumes from 1881 to 1922. At the same time, Elizabeth controversially organized a committee of female scholars for what she described as "a thorough revision of the Old and New Testaments, and to ascertain what the status of woman really was under the Jewish and Christian religion."[71]

Her release of Part I of *The Woman's Bible* in November 1895 received a flurry of clergy denunciations and media criticism. *The Woman's Bible* emerged from Elizabeth's discontented belief that all religions taught women's inferiority and subjection. In her autobiography, Elizabeth confessed that she had "sedulously labored to rouse women to a realization of their degraded position in the Church, and presented resolutions at every annual convention for that purpose."[72]

She preached from the London pulpit of freethinking Unitarian minister Moncure D. Conway in 1882 in an address themed, "What has Christianity done for Woman?" Elizabeth told the congregation, "Whatever heights of dignity and purity women have individually attained, can in no way be attributed to the dogmas of their religion."[73] Her radical religious beliefs ultimately divided the woman's rights movement and distanced members of the Suffrage Association.

Elizabeth addressed the National Suffrage Association Convention of 1890, saying, "I hope this convention will declare that the Woman Suffrage Association is opposed to all union of Church and State, and pledges itself as far

---

[71]   Ibid., 390.
[72]   Ibid., 382.
[73]   Ibid., 357.

as possible to maintain the secular nature of our Government."[74] Susan's speech likewise confirmed the irrelevance of religious creed to the movement: "If it is necessary, I will fight forty years more to make our platform free for the Christian to stand upon, whether she be a Catholic and counts her beads, or a Protestant of the straightest orthodox sect, just as I have fought for the rights of the 'infidels' the last forty years. These are the principles I want to maintain—that our platform may be kept as broad as the universe, that upon it may stand the representatives of all creeds and of no creeds—Jew and Christian, Protestant and Catholic, Gentile and Mormon, believer and atheist."[75]

Sacred Motherhood

In an article published in the liberal political magazine *The Arena* in 1894, Elizabeth wrote, "The contradictory views in which woman is represented are as pitiful as varied. While the Magnificat to the Virgin is chanted in all our cathedrals round the globe on each returning Sabbath day, and her motherhood extolled by her worshipers, maternity for the rest of womankind is referred to as a weakness, a disability, a curse, an evidence of woman's divinely ordained subjection. Yet surely the real woman should have some points of resemblance in character and position with the ideal one, whom poets, novelists, and artists portray."[76] In her desperation to reconcile motherhood with its extolled position, as

---

[74]   *VOTES FOR WOMEN,* 3051.
[75]   *VOTES FOR WOMEN,* 3053.
[76]   Ibid., 230.

evidenced by the Mother of God, Elizabeth glimpsed the Catholic understanding that "the secret of making speedy progress in achieving full respect for women and their identity involves more than simply the condemnation of discrimination and injustices," as was said by St. John Paul II in his 1995 *Letter to Women*. He said it must begin "with a *universal recognition of the dignity of women*."[77]

Elizabeth, who became a mother at the age of twenty-seven, watched her family grow until delivering her seventh child, Robert, at the age of forty-four. She reflected in her autobiography, "Though motherhood is the most important of all the professions,—requiring more knowledge than any other department in human affairs,—yet there is not sufficient attention given to the preparation for this office."[78] Realizing throughout her years of travel that few women knew how to care for babies, her public transportation commutes often became a comical classroom in motherhood.

Elizabeth often contradicted the absurd medical advice of doctors and baby books of her day. "My advice to every mother is, above all other arts and sciences, study first what relates to babyhood, as there is no department of human action in which there is such lamentable ignorance," she wrote.[79] Having little faith in the popular theories on babies, she recalled that "when we hold in our arms for the first time, a being of infinite possibilities, in whose wisdom may rest the destiny of a nation, we take it for granted that the laws governing its life, health, and happiness are intuitively

---

[77]   John Paul II, *Letter of Pope John Paul II to Women*, June 29, 1995.
[78]   Ibid., 112.
[79]   Ibid., 121.

understood, that there is nothing new to be learned in regard to it."[80]

Susan referred to motherhood as a sacred domain in her famous 1875 *Social Purity* lecture. She declared that a new order of goodness would be known when "the mother of Christ shall be made the true model of womanhood and motherhood."[81] She believed that humanity would be redeemed through women, moving past the repetitive process of women being condemned to dependence. She desired women to know independent self-support and discover their own personal joy.

Susan believed that mothers would ensure the future greatness of the nation, saying, "To hold mothers responsible for the character of their sons while you deny them any control over the surroundings of their lives, is worse than mockery, it is cruelty! Responsibilities grow out of rights and powers. . . . [Mothers] must possess all possible rights and powers to control the conditions and circumstances of their own and their children's lives."[82] Susan B. Anthony became the political and social mother of many through her sincere friendship and mentorship of countless women. She was fierce in the political ring and a maternal guiding force in the world.

---

[80]   Ibid., 113.
[81]   Harper, *The Life and Work of Susan B. Anthony*, vol. II, 1011.
[82]   Ibid., 1011–12.

Abortion – Nineteenth Century

"Abortion before marriage and especially after marriage are the rule rather than the exception—in the wealthy and fashionable classes, and to a great extent among workingwomen who say they 'can't afford to have children.' Many women learn to practice it on themselves, and many of them have repeated it dozens of times; and unprofessional gentlemen by the score, boast confidentially to their friends that 'they can do it as well as the doctors.' The majority of women, as a result of all these causes, and other faults in our methods of living, have the abominable [STD], and even little girls are dying by the hundred from diseases which in other ages of the world were only known, if at all, among the most debauched and profligate women."[83]

—Tennessee Claflin, 1871

Few issues are as morally divisive as abortion. But, until my teens, abortion was foreign to me. I had received my early sacraments in the Catholic Church and attended Sunday Mass for the first thirteen years of my life. But I wasn't *taught* the Faith, and my faith was empty. My brother and I went one night a week, with other public-school kids,

---

[83] Tennie C. Claflin, "MY WORD ON ABORTION, AND OTHER THINGS," *Woodhull and Claflin's Weekly*, vol. 3, no. 19, Sept. 23, 1871, 9.

to a Catholic religious education program. For many of us, the program seemed like an unnecessary extension of our school day and did little to help us face the weighty moral challenges we were already encountering. Instead, my atheist and agnostic peers became my most relevant teachers on the passionate abortion debate, which seemed obviously defendable in dire circumstances.

The girls who became pregnant in our high school reflected our worst fears, of being judged and pitied by our peers and isolated from the class. The pregnant girls who took care of their "problem" were back to school by the end of the week, their abortion nothing more than a sob story among other tales of breakups and bad relationships. I remember learning, over tears, that one of my high school friends had gotten an abortion over the weekend. She graduated at the end of the year with the rest of us, and none but her closest friends ever knew about her abortion. By high school standards in the absence of moral formation, all that mattered was the undoing of an unwanted situation. What did we know of or care about regret? Abortion wasn't a choice; it was an escape, and we all wanted access to that escape route.

Giving it as little thought as possible, I settled on a socially agreeable platform. Although I couldn't imagine aborting my own child, I felt that I had no right to make that judgement for any other woman. Looking back to that time, I didn't know what abortion was. I didn't know that a human person was being aborted and I didn't know the methods abortionists employed. If I'm honest with myself, I didn't *want* to know, if that meant forfeiting my membership to the global feminist club. But, one day, as I drove down the main highway of our small town, the traffic slowed and gave way to a crowd of people chanting and holding up signs of aborted babies. They stood several blocks deep as they crowded to the edges of the road, waving their visually shocking signs. Regardless of the initial repulsion I felt toward their radical display, I couldn't look away. An image caught my eye and was seared into my consciousness: the image of a full-term baby's head covered in dark hair, grasped tightly between forceps, and detached from its body. "What *is* that?" I asked myself, horrified as the human reality hit me. And suddenly, at that moment, I knew: *That's* abortion.

Shockingly, before there was a definable "feminist" movement, abortion had deep roots and was frequented in the nineteenth century by the rich as much as the poor. According to author and historian Clifford Browder, in his 1988 book *The Wickedest Woman in New York,* "the dramatic midcentury upsurge in abortion was largely due to reputable married women who 'turned to it because they found frequent childbearing physically or financially burdensome, unfashionable, or socially inconvenient.'" Browder reported a study done in 1868 projecting that one New York pregnancy in five ended in abortion, "an estimate that left vast numbers of undetected cases out of the account."[84] Dr. Horatio Storer, who formed the nineteenth-century Committee on Criminal Abortion, produced early statistics on abortion, which was the focus of his research. Accounting for the disproportionate increase in stillbirths in New York

---

[84]   Clifford Browder, *The Wickedest Woman in New York* (Archon Books, 1988), 127.

city in 1868, Storer found that "the reported early abortions, of which the greater number of course escape registry, bear the ratio to the living births of 1 in 4.04, while elsewhere they are only 1 in 78.5."[85] Abortion was far more common among American Protestants than Catholic immigrants, who often payed the price of frequent childbirths with perpetual poverty and inescapable stigma.

Abortion has since become synonymous with feminism. The National Organization for Women (NOW), founded in 1966 under President Betty Friedan, declared in their October 29, 1966 Statement of Purpose, "The time has come to confront, with concrete action, the conditions that now prevent women from enjoying . . . freedom of choice which is their right."[86] NOW claims to be "the largest feminist activist organization in the United States" and "affirms that reproductive rights are issues of life and death for women, not mere matters of choice."[87] Most twenty-first-century American feminists proudly unite their beliefs with NOW and Planned Parenthood, claiming reproductive rights—including abortion and contraception—as foundational for the movement's platform of personal freedom and sexual sovereignty. Distinguishing yourself as a "pro-life feminist" requires clarification as to how two seemingly contradictory

---

[85]   Horatio Robinson Store, *Criminal Abortion: Its Nature, Its Evidence, and Its Law* (Boston: Little Brown, and Company, 1868), 34.

[86]   "Statement of Purpose," *National Organization for Women*, https://now.org/about/history/statement-of-purpose/, accessed April, 25, 2020.

[87]   "Our Issues," *National Organization for Women*, https://now.org/about/our-issues/, accessed April, 25, 2020.

philosophies can coexist and courage to challenge the defensive passion and power of lobbying that swell around this issue.

Madame Restell

In 1847, an anonymous New York physician wrote about the harrowing conditions that faced unwed American mothers in his account of Madame Restell. He reported:

> The woman who becomes a mother, when unmarried, here passes a fiery ordeal, from which she shrinks with terror. If she makes known her condition, a public disgrace awaits her: if she tries to conceal it, she is liable to imprisonment, Society frowns upon her – the laws bring all their terrors. What is the result? . . . The fruit of our rigid virtue is infanticide, murder, and of late, Restellism – a name now fittingly bestowed, in some of our public prints, upon the procurement of abortion, by such medical and mechanical means as are said to be practiced by Restell.[88]

Madame Restell was perhaps the most fascinating and influential character in abortion history. Her legacy forever shaped our preconception of abortion, it influenced monumental laws, and changed our prejudice of who were giving and getting abortions. We know her as the most profitable and notorious abortionist of the nineteenth century, rising from poverty to enormous success in the business of

---

[88]   *Life of Madame Restell, with an account of Her Professional Career, and Secret Practices* (New York: Charles V. Smith, 1847), 7.

abortion and contraception. She was the heroine of men seeking to escape responsibility for an unplanned pregnancy and the procurer of contraceptive powders to overwhelmed mothers, who often returned for an abortion when the powders proved ineffective. But Madame Restell wasn't who she said she was. Untrained in medicine, she and her husband Charles Lohman, whom *The New York Sun* referred to as "the most successful quack in the history of the city," both operated under fraudulent medical titles.[89] Even so, Madame Restell was so well known to the public that her last name became synonymous with abortion. "Restellism" frequently appeared as a term for abortion throughout nineteenth-century newspaper advertisements, diaries, women's rights debates, and legal trials.

George Washington Dixon, the inflammatory New York editor of the *Polyanthos*, labelled her "The Wickedest Woman in New York,"[90] while the *National Police Gazette* designated her "The Female Abortionist" and caricatured her as a scowling young woman rising from a bat-like demon devouring a baby. Caroline Ann Trow, born in England in 1812, became a maid at age fifteen and teenage bride and widow shortly after. With her husband and daughter, Ann sailed to America in 1831, settling in Manhattan. However, she was forced to support herself and her daughter as a seamstress when her husband died suddenly.

Her dark features and ambitious nature soon caught the attention of Charles Lohman, a printer at the *New York*

---

89   *The New York Sun*, Monday, April 1, 1918, 14.
90   *Polyanthos*, February 20, 1841.

Herald, and the two married in 1836. Through mixing with other radical freethinkers and philosophers, Charles opened a new world to Ann. Promoting works of socialists and atheists, Charles was particularly interested in contraceptive methods for population control. He championed the radical works of Robert Dale Owen's *Moral Physiology* (1831), Charles Knowlton's *Fruits of Philosophy* (1832), and the *Free Enquirer*, a weekly journal by Owen and Frances Wright criticizing religion, slavery, and suffrage, and advocating birth control.

Faux Physicians

As immigrants, Ann and Charles both largely invested in the American dream, desiring to move up in status and wealth by any means possible. Not possessing religious convictions, Ann scandalized a visiting committee of women from the *Advocate of Moral Reform* when they came to her prison cell in 1841, saying, "I fear neither God or man, nor care for heaven or hell!"[91] Convinced of the lucrative possibilities of selling birth control, Ann and Charles embarked on a scandalous medical and pharmaceutical business. They began marketing patent medicines for women in need of preventing and ending pregnancies, and eventually both operated as self-styled New York physicians, delivering babies and performing abortions.

The United States followed British common-law until 1828, which stated that abortion before quickening, or fetal

---

[91]   *The Advocate of Moral Reform,* vol. VII, no. 9, New York, May 1, 1841, 71.

movement, was neither morally nor legally wrong. However, even after introducing these abortion provisions and despite the outcry of credible medical doctors against fake doctors, "New York's 1827 law against unauthorized physicians and its 1828 abortion law both remained unenforced."[92] In the absence of upholding regulations and requiring medical licensure, many quacks began to advertise and practice as physicians. Preposterous claims were made by "doctors" who invented uncorroborated histories of studying at medical schools and practicing in hospitals across Europe. New York was so clouded with quack doctors that the public couldn't distinguish between those who were authentic and fake.

One such quack, Dr. William Evans, lived next door to the Lohmans in Manhattan. His advertisements regularly boasted cures for anything from a cough to consumption. Operating as a personal drug compounder, Evans began performing abortions in 1838. He likely taught Ann and Charles his compounding and abortion techniques before Ann launched her "medical" career in 1839.[93] After discovering great success in selling contraceptive formulas, Ann and Charles expanded their business in March 1840 to include a (maternity/abortion) lying-in-hospital on Greenwich Street. They listed themselves in the *City Directory* as Caroline Restell, physician, and Charles Lohman, publisher.

Under the very eloquent and witty pen of her husband, Ann began to place advertisements in all prominent newspapers. She chose the alias Restell, claiming to be the protegee

---

92   Browder, *The Wickedest Woman in New York*, 14.
93   Ibid., 7.

and granddaughter of a French physician named Madame Restell. One of her first advertisements in *The New York Morning Herald* claimed that her contraceptive powders "have been used in Europe with invariable success, (first introduced by the celebrated Midwife and Female Physician, Madame Restell, the grandmother of the advertiser, who made this subject her particular and especial study.)"[94] But the existence of a French midwife/abortionist named Madame Restell and any relation to Ann are unfounded.

This didn't stop her, however, from using the mysterious French "expert" to fool the public and the law. Ann opened a New York medical practice and boarding house under the title *"Madame Restell, Female Physician,"* while continuing to allege to be practicing under a senior Restell, in France. An 1842 advertisement in the *New York Herald* claimed that Restell's Preventative Powders were discovered in 1808, before Ann was born. It assured the public in print that "Madame Restell, as is well known, was for thirty years Female Physician in the two principle Female Hospitals in Europe – those of Vienna and Paris."[95] Ann continued this charade for the rest of her life, denying the alias when questioned directly by a judge and responding to a skeptical editorial by Samuel Jenks Smith, saying, "I have not changed my name, and that the person who assists me answers to my name during my absence, it being impossible for me to attend all my business

---

94   *The New York Morning Herald*, vol. V., no. 278, Monday, April 13, 1840.

95   *The New York Herald*, vol. VIII., no. 281, Tuesday, October 11, 1842, 4.

myself."[96] Charles furthered the deception by releasing a statement in the *Herald* that Madame Restell was a lady of about seventy-five years old, who had authorized others to act on her behalf.[97]

The "Mother" of Abortion

Was Ann "Restell" Lohman's only real crime that she deceived the public and the law, in hopes of fortune, as many others had done? Multiple feminist accounts of Madame Restell paint her as an unsung hero of her time—a woman who took matters into her own hands by bringing relief to over-burdened mothers and freedom to unwed mothers facing detrimental public shame. She established a pregnancy clinic, maternity home, adoption center, and abortion facil-ity all in one. But this is far from the truth. Caroline Ann Trow Lohman was a fraud whose ambition for financial gain caused her to risk the lives of many women. She publicly advertised and practiced as a knowledgeable and trusted pharmacist and physician. She took advantage of desper-ate clients who returned for intrusive abortions when her prescribed abortifacients failed—"$20 for a poor woman, $100 for a wealthy one."[98] Catering to the rich, she moved her practice uptown to West Broadway, where there was no shortage of wealthy clients. The Lohmans were offered financial comfort, prestigious connections, and in working

---

96   *The New York Morning Herald*, vol. V., no. 156, July 15, 1839.
97   Browder, *The Wickedest Woman in New York*, 28.
98   Ibid., 16.

with the most well-known New York families, the assurance of secrecy.

Did Restell care at all for the well-being of her clients or the progress of women in society? As she and Charles brokered deals with the husbands and boyfriends of heart-broken and emotionally unstable women, it's hard to believe that she cared for anything more than her bank account. Cordelia A. Grant, a victim of the Lohmans, gave her testimony in court, stating that her common-law husband of seven years had insisted and arranged for her five abortions, three at the hands of Restell, despite her refusals, "so that my health and constitution are broken and greatly impaired."[99] Another client named Anne Dahl was sold thirty-one abortifacient pills in June 1839, and after suffering a bad reaction, she contacted her physician and the police. But charges against Restell were dropped when Anne Dahl died destitute of puerperal fever, a rapidly progressing bacterial infection in the genital tract, nine months later. She was buried in the potter's field. Despite the unknown formula of Restell's Preventative Powders and one potential death attributed to her in the first year, six outlets for distribution cropped up in the city, as well as in Providence, Newark, Philadelphia, and Boston by January 1, 1840. All customers returning for an abortion were referred to Restell's main office in New York.

Of her 1841 trial for the death of one of her patients, Mary Ann Purdy, George Washington Dixon wrote, "Within a year Madame Restell has procured several hundred abortions,"[100]

---

[99]   *New York Daily Times*, February 14, 1854, 1.

[100]   "Trial of Madame Restell, Alias Ann Lohman, for Abortion and Causing the Death of Mrs. Purdy: Being a Full Account of All the

and angrily declared, "Bring a few Madame Restell's into the country, and there would be no need of axe, or gallows, or any other check on population. . . . According to her own account, six acres of sod would not cover the work she has done in New-York alone in a single year."[101] Purdy gave her testimony from her deathbed, stating that on June 2, 1839, she was sold a small vial of yellow liquid by Restell. After suffering an adverse reaction, Purdy had the vial analyzed by Dr. David D. Marvin of Greenwich Street. In *The Wickedest Woman in New York*, Browder writes, "Analysis on one occasion revealed the pills were composed of ergot and cantharides, or Spanish fly, and on another that a fluid sold by her contained oil of tansy and spirits of turpentine, which the analyst considered dangerous."[102] Still, Purdy desperately returned to Restell on July 20 for an abortion. She was led behind a curtain into a darkened room and made to lie on a blanket on the floor, where a man (Lohman), rather than Restell, performed the procedure. Purdy miscarried three days later but retained the afterbirth for over a week. This caused her health to decline during the next year and a half, and she died a week after Restell was indicted by the grand jury on April 21, 1841.

The Ann Lohman (Restell) trial was the first highly publicized abortion case in the country, pronouncing a guilty verdict on July 20, 1841. Sensationalism surrounding the trial overtook the news media, inspiring even Edgar Allen

---

Proceedings on the Trial, Together with the Suppressed Evidence and Editorial Remarks," New York, 1841, 5.

[101]   Ibid., 7.
[102]   Browder, *The Wickedest Woman in New York*, 16.

Poe to write a fictional story, *The Mystery of Marie Rogêt*, in which is suggested a botched abortion when the body of a young woman named Mary Rogers was discovered floating in the Hudson River, just days after the trial. Restell's indictment was finally dropped on February 12, 1844, by the State Supreme Court, since her appeal for a new trial was impossible, considering the chief witness was dead.

During this time, Dr. Gunning S. Bedford, a distinguished professor of obstetrics and founder of the University Medical College in New York, reported urgently treating another patient of Restell's named Eliza Merritt. Inspired by his Catholic faith, Bedford established the first obstetrical clinic for the poor, responding to patients unable to afford care. Eliza Merritt had been experiencing severe labor pains for fourteen hours, and an examination proved that inflicted injuries to her womb had sealed its opening, making it impossible for her to deliver her child. Bedford performed on her the first successful case of a vaginal hysterotomy (incision into the uterus through the vagina) recorded in the United States on December 19, 1843. Due to the success of the procedure, Bedford published the case in *The New York Journal of Medicine*, March 1844, also exposing Restell, whom he called a "monster," to the medical community:

> About six weeks after becoming pregnant, she called on the notorious Madame Restell, who, learning her situation, gave her some powders with directions for use; these powders, it appears, did not produce the desired effect. She returned again to this woman, and asked her if there were no other way to make her miscarry.

"Yes," says Madame Restell, "I can probe you; but I must have my price for this operation." "What do you probe with?" "A piece of whalebone." "Well," observed the patient, "I cannot afford to pay your price, and I will probe myself." She returned home and used the whalebone several times; it produced considerable pain, followed by discharge of blood.

Madame Restell, on previous occasions, had caused her to miscarry five times, and that these miscarriages had, in every instance, been brought about by drugs administered by this trafficker in human life. The only case in which the medicines failed was the last pregnancy, when at the suggestion of Madame Restell, she probed herself, and induced the condition of things described, and which most seriously involved her own safety, as well as that of her child. In the course of conversation, this woman mentioned that she knew a great number of persons who were in the habit of applying to Madame Restell for the purpose of miscarrying, and that she scarcely ever failed in affording the desired relief; and among others, she cited the case of a female residing in Houston-street, who was five months pregnant; Madame Restell probed her, and she was delivered of a child, to use her own expression, "that kicked several times after it was put into the bowl."[103]

Restell remained seemingly impervious to the growing media hype surrounding her. Despite a career littered with arrests,

---

[103]   Nicolas Charles Chailly-Honoré, *A Practical Treatise on Midwifery* (New York: Harper & Brothers, 1851), 303–4.

detentions, and trials, Restell's growing wealth and connection often ensured her a speedy release on bail, becoming a sore subject on the unjust persuasion of money in cases of the rich. New York passed a law on May 13, 1845, making the death of either the woman or the fetus after quickening second-degree manslaughter and punishable by four to seven years in the state prison. Attempted abortion was declared criminal at any stage, also subjecting assistants and pharmacists to three to twelve months in jail. Two years later, in 1847, Restell was found guilty, without bail, in the case of Maria Bodine, who was six months pregnant when Restell performed an abortion on her, which left her crippled. Maria Bodine's haunting account of her abortion displayed but one of the strange instances of Restell insisting that her clients use the endearing term "mother" in addressing her:

> "Madame Restell inserted her hand in my privates, and said it would make it easier for me; it gave me more pain; every pain I had I heard something fall from my body into the stool or chamber. . . . Madame Restell again inserted her hand; she hurt me so, I hallooed out and gripped hold of her hand; she told me to have patience, and I would call her mother for it." When asked to see her child, Restell said to Maria, "it was not worth while; she would not; and she put it behind the fire place, saying she would remove it at night."[104]

Despite the testimony of doctors such as Bedford, who argued against the common law distinction between fetal

---

[104] *Wonderful Trial of Caroline Lohman, Alias Restell, with Speeches of Counsel, Charge of Court, and Verdict of Jury*, 3rd ed., (New York: 1847), 7.

life before and after quickening, due to continual gestational development, the law disagreed. Bedford opposed abortion at any stage, as it was condemned by the Hippocratic oath and opposed to his reverence for human life in any form.[105] In his court testimony, Bedford said, "Physicians consider that life is perfect in the earlier months, the earliest, in fact of pregnancy, and that the child is as much alive then, as at any subsequent period." Brady, Restell's lawyer, answered, "Yes, but lawyers do not; there is a distinction between what you regard as life – natural life, and legal life."[106]

Restell was charged with a misdemeanor in *The People v. Caroline Lohman, alias Ann Lohman, alias Madame Restell,* and sent to the penitentiary on Blackwell (Roosevelt) Island for a year. Using her wealth and connections to ensure a comfortable stay, Restell slept on a feather rather than straw bed. She received her meals from the warden's table and the distinct privilege of using his office instead of participating in the communal work required of inmates. She brokered unsupervised visits with Charles and paid prisoners to clean her cell, do her washing, and make clothing for her. The grand jury nodded at the systematic favoritism but did little to remedy it.

Meanwhile, Joseph Trow, Restell's younger brother, came from England to assist in the compounding business, while Charles made the overnight switch of professions from publisher to physician. Charles published a book under the alias Dr. A. M. Mauriceau in 1847 titled *The Married Woman's*

---

105   Browder, *The Wickedest Woman in New York,* 48–49.
106   *Wonderful Trial,* 17.

Private Medical Companion. Quoting physicians and borrowing heavily from radical reformers Robert Dale Owen and Charles Knowlton, the book promoted contraception, using bold and colorful language to address menstruation, pregnancy, miscarriage, abortion, barrenness, and sterility. Charles argued, "That the instinct of reproduction should be, like our other appetites and passions, subject to the control of reason, - that when the gratification of this instinct results in evil effects . . . if such evil can be prevented, it is the obligation of morality that it should be."[107]

Littered with self-serving advertisements carefully hidden in the footnotes, Charles promoted compounds that "neutralize the fecundating properties in semen . . . and maintains the elasticity and firmness of the generative functions."[108] He introduced the condom, suggesting that in addition to avoiding syphilis in prostitution, "a covering (used by the male), called a *baudruche* (known as the French Secret), is used with success in preventing pregnancy."[109] He further claimed that the dangers of abortion "are often magnified and exaggerated," stating that he, "in the course of his practice as Professor of the Diseases of Women, has been called upon to effect miscarriages, and in all cases, it has proved perfectly safe."[110]

Charles spent four nights in jail for the publication of an obscene book, after which he began operating full time

---

[107] A. M. Mauriceau, *The Married Woman's Private Medical Companion*, 146.
[108] Ibid., 142.
[109] Ibid., 144.
[110] Ibid., 169.

under the alias Dr. A. M. Mauriceau, Professor of Diseases of Women, claiming to have studied medicine abroad and to have assisted in France under M. P. Dubios,[111] "the oracle of French midwifery."[112] But as Browder pointed out in *The Wickedest Woman in New York*, "The author's name, his pretensions to years of medical experience in France, and his much-vaulted medicines were fake."[113]

The Heart Is Deceitful Above All Things

Restell's "adoption process" was equally appalling and includes two documented cases of malpractice and abduction. Mary Applegate's story captured the heart of the public, who followed her sad saga of becoming pregnant by a wealthy stockbroker named Augustus Edwards. Applegate's sworn testimony on February 5, 1846, appeared in the *New York Tribune*, alleging that after arranging for her board, Applegate spent the last four weeks of her pregnancy at Restell's Greenwich Street home.[114] During this time, Applegate was repeatedly pressured by Restell, who wanted Applegate's baby for an adoption client. Despite Applegate's refusal, Restell tried in vain to convince Applegate of the good living she could make prostituting herself in the city to men "who would be glad to 'keep'" her and allow her to "dress well and live in great style," according to the published accounts in

---

[111]   Ibid., 181.
[112]   Nicolas Charles Chailly-Honoré, *A Practical Treatise on Midwifery*, 1.
[113]   Browder, *The Wickedest Woman in New York*, 73.
[114]   *The New York Daily Tribune*, no. 258, February 6, 1846.

the *Tribune* and the 1846 edition of the American journal *The New York Medical and Surgical Reporter*.[115]

On December 11, 1845, Applegate birthed a baby girl, whom Restell took away screaming, despite Applegate's pleas for her child. The following day, Applegate held her child briefly before Restell removed and placed her in the care of a nurse, Catharine Rider. Applegate appealed to Augustus Edwards, the baby's father, who confronted Restell. But Restell denied any association with Mary Applegate and claimed that no female child had been born at her residence for several months.[116] Sadly, despite her extensive search and vain legal attempts, Mary Applegate never saw her baby again.

Similarly, Restell was arrested in 1856 for the abduction of another boarder's child. Frederica W. Medinger testified that Restell delivered her baby on August 30, 1855, and despite her pleas, Medinger never saw her son again. Although Restell alleged that Frederica "freely and voluntarily surrendered him" to be adopted, the Supreme Court ruled otherwise on April 21, 1856. Restell was given ten days to offer an account of the child. But justice was foiled once again as no answer ever came. In fact, no court record remains, after the judge's initial ruling, and nothing was ever heard of Frederica Medinger again. Some suggest the Lohmans wielded their monetary power and high-profile connections to keep Federica quiet.

---

[115]   *The New York Medical and Surgical Reporter* (New York: Piercy & Reed, 1846), 159.

[116]   *The New York Medical and Surgical Reporter*, 160.

By 1860, the notorious Madame, who was called "mother" by the "daughters" of New York, along with her husband Charles, had gained all the wealth and fortune they had originally set out to attain in their early compounding days. Building their empire on the sin and the shame of wealthy New York families, the Lohmans moved further uptown. They invested in prized real estate on upper Fifth Avenue and built a residential mansion near Central Park. The Lohmans were close enough to the construction site of Saint Patrick's Cathedral to create scandal, outbidding the archbishop on ten lots he wanted for his official residence. Their exquisite four-story brownstone rose atop its basement office at a cost of $200,000, over $6 million today, with additional lavish details such as $28,000 stables, $20,000 worth of Italian frescoes, and decadent ornamentals, including a $3,000 Parisian rug.

Yet, as the extravagant mansion was completed, family relationships crumbled. Two of their four grandchildren died. Their daughter Carrie moved in after her first marriage failed. Shortly thereafter, she and her mother severed their relationship permanently. Restell's brother, Joseph, also bitterly ended his relationship and long partnership with the Lohmans with a lawsuit to recover $10,000 in bonds. Restell's two remaining grandchildren moved back into the mansion as teenagers, and when Charles died of kidney disease in 1877, they became her sole heirs.

Restell continued practicing her profession from the basement of her mansion, serving only the wealthy: "By one account, $500 a case; by another, from $200 to 2,000 – at a time when obscure practitioners in the provinces were charging as little as $10," according to Browder.[117] Remaining careful in her practice, Restell seemed unfazed by the stricter New York abortion laws, which banned advertisements alluding to abortion and birth control in 1868 and sought to ban the sale of abortion-inducing material in 1872. But the Comstock Law of 1873, which made it illegal to use the US Postal Service to transmit any obscene and morally illicit product or information, laid the final trap to catch her.

Anthony Comstock built a career against vice—specifically prostitution, pornography, and birth control advertising and distribution—and was ultimately responsible for the final undoing of Restell. As agent and secretary to the New York Society for the Suppression of Vice, Comstock never tired of bringing to account pornographers and abortionists. "The message of these evil things is death – socially, morally, physically, and spiritually," he wrote in his 1883 book *Traps for the Youth*.[118]

A year after Charles Lohman's death, Restell was tricked into selling Comstock abortifacients and offering him her abortion services. Comstock arrested her on February 23, 1878, as she prepared for another round of charades in court. But this time, due to her advanced age and without the help of Charles, Restell found the trials long and her confinement agonizing. Her grandson struggled to get patron supporters from the community, which quickly disowned her. She also followed the scornful public resentment toward her in the

---

117 Browder, *The Wickedest Woman in New York*, 125.
118 Anthony Comstock, *Traps for the Youth*, 4th Ed. (New York and London: Funk & Wagnalls Co., 1883), 131.

newspapers, all of which proved to be too overwhelming for the sixty-seven-year-old abortionist.

Those wishing ill of the devious Madame Restell were eventually satisfied when at last she met a dark end to her life on April Fools' Day. Ann Lohman, alias Madame Restell, previously undeterred and untouchable by the justice system, slit her throat in the bathtub of her mansion on the morning of her trial in 1878, becoming Comstock's fifteenth offender to be driven to suicide.[119] As a New York physician wrote in 1847:

> It was in such a community as this, that a woman of the profession of Madame Restell might have expected to flourish, precisely because it is less moral than it wishes to appear, and because where there is only the appearance of virtue, vice, to be active, only asks impunity. This has been, and is the case in New York, and to a greater or less extent, every where. [Services for unwed mothers] are confessions of weakness. They say, we are weak – we are frail – we are liable to go astray; and this is the remedy we provide – while here, we confess no weakness, we provide no remedies, and behold, the consequence, in a damning public infamy, like this business of Restell.[120]

119   Browder, *The Wickedest Woman in New York*, 188.
120   *Life of Madame Restell*, 7–8.

What Say the Suffragettes on Abortion?

The heated abortion and "reproductive rights" debates now synonymous with feminism also registered with Susan B. Anthony and her contemporaries. The fight for human dignity and equality of all people under the law was one the suffragettes lived intimately in an America steeped in slavery and structured to deny women the vote. Sexuality, promiscuity, contraception, and abortion may have been hidden from the public eye in nineteenth-century America, but they certainly weren't foreign to society. The early activists had quite a lot to say about abortion and contraception, and they recognized the unborn child's rights among the injustices worth correcting by women's rights advocates.

Radical suffragette Victoria Woodhull was a trailblazer on several fronts. She became the first woman to run for president in the 1872 election against Grant, she gained notoriety for her multiple marriages and lovers, and she actively promoted the idea of free love. Despite her radical beliefs on sexuality, however, Woodhull and her sister, Tennessee Claflin, were outspoken opponents of abortion. Starting their own socialist newspaper called *Woodhull & Claflin's Weekly* from the proceeds they made on Wall Street as the first female stockbrokers, the sisters regularly spoke their mind.

Victoria made abortion the subject of a special editorial she published on August 8, 1870, titled "*When is it Not Murder to Take Life?*" When challenged by *The Hartford Courant* on her opinion of the notorious abortionist Madame Restell, Victoria stated, "Whoever has read the WEEKLY knows I hold abortion (except to save the life of the mother) to be just as much murder as the killing of a person after birth is murder."[121]

Victoria and Tennessee reported often on abortion in their paper, challenging the double standard and faulting the suicide, murder, and abortion of the mothers of illegitimate children on society. They found the disgrace and burden heaped upon these women, disowned by family and shunned from social life, to be unforgivable, writing in their paper in 1872: "Here legal motherhood is creditable, hence illegal motherhood begets disgrace, and hence suicide and murder. When the day comes that motherhood is deemed the right of all healthy women, and no disgrace attaches to the manner of it, then murder and abortion will cease, and not until then."[122]

Tennessee echoed the voice of many suffragettes on abortion. She rarely blamed as much as pitied the women who were reduced to choosing this unnatural and moral evil. The suffragettes identified abortion as a flawed symptom of the social state, which, in refusing women the rights to be self-sufficient, therefore abandoned them to such dire straits

---

[121]   *Victoria C. Woodhull*, "To the Editor of the Hartford Courant," *Woodhull and Claflin's Weekly*, vol. 4, no. 3, Dec 2, 1871, 9.

[122]   "PRESS JUSTICE," *Woodhull and Claflin's Weekly*, vol. 4, no. 19, Mar 23, 1872, 9.

as abortion. Tennessee addressed this in a powerfully moving and witty piece published in the *Weekly's* September 23, 1871 issue; *MY WORD ON ABORTION, AND OTHER THINGS*: "Abortion is only a symptom of a more deep-seated disorder of the social state. It cannot be put down by law. Normally the mother of ten children is as healthy, and may be as youthful and beautiful, as a healthy maiden. Child-bearing is not a disease, but a beautiful office of nature. But to our faded-out, sickly, exhausted type of women, it is a fearful ordeal. Nearly every child born is an unwelcome guest. Abortion is the choice of evils for such women."[123]

Tennessee was appalled by the wealthy New York men of Wall Street and Broad Street who boosted abortion's prevalence by bringing their own daughters and female friends to wealthy practitioners like Madame Restell each year to cover up their "difficulty." Tennessee asked the rhetorical question, "Who really wants that there should be no opportunity to secure an abortion *under peculiarly trying circumstances?*"[124] She posed the question to the wealthy and fashionable classes, observing that "abortion before marriage and especially after marriage are the rule rather than the exception," and to the "workingwomen who say they 'can't afford to have children.'" Tennessee's point was that very few people with the power to rightfully change the social disorder of abortion really wanted to due to their personal benefit. She criticized this cultural acceptance of abortion, writing in 1871 that abortion was "one of the indicative symptoms

---

[123]   Claflin, 9.
[124]   Ibid.

of the ripening and the rottening of our prevalent state of society."[125]

It wasn't only men who Tennessee found deplorable in bringing mistresses and daughters to abortionists but married wealthy women as well, who secured multiple abortions for themselves in order to avoid personal inconvenience. Tennessee abhorred the way these women senselessly existed with such a reckless lack of meaning. She saw the unhappy example of these upper-class women further contributing to the idea that motherhood was a dreaded burden, preferring abortion to life. "But the great revenue of these practitioners is from the married women among the wealthy. The lives of dissipation and senseless inanity which these women lead; the oppressions and disgusts of the marriage state; their hopeless and aimless lives; all together have so depressed the nervous energy of our women that they dread beyond endurance the burdens of child-bearing and the care of children. They have become unfit to have children, and abortion is the sewerage for this wretched stagnation of feminine life."[126]

It's amazing that someone like Tennessee Claflin—a childhood abuse survivor who overcame poverty, worked as a clairvoyant, began the first female brokerage firm backed by Cornelius Vanderbilt, and was the first to publish *The Communist Manifesto* in English in her own newspaper—also wrote such clear-headed and poignant accounts of abortion and its negative effects on social motherhood. Tennessee didn't propose that abortion could be undone by repression

---

[125]   Ibid.
[126]   Ibid.

and law. Rather, her solution was greater freedom in the social sphere and teaching physiology to women, declaring in her paper in 1871, "It will be when women are thrown on their own resources, when they mingle on more equal terms with men, when they are aroused to enterprise and developed in their intellects; when, in a word, a new sort of life is devised through freedom, that we can recover the lost ground of true virtue, coupled with the advantages of the most advanced age."[127]

Tennessee passionately spoke out against mothers subjecting their daughters to inherit willful ignorance and proprietary shame of the mechanics of her female anatomy. Instead, she pointed out that young girls often learned these things in the wrong ways from school companions and were just as easily crushed by gossip for their curiosity. Shamed from learning and discussing matters of her anatomy, the health of young girls was compromised. They fearfully entered marriage and childbearing with little understanding of its natural process.

Physiology and the Birds and the Bees

I encountered a searing moment of humiliation in fifth grade that clarifies Tennessee Claflin's wisdom in advocating for young women to be taught about their bodies. The beauty and innocence of my childhood allowed me to reach fifth grade as a naïve dreamer, ignorant of physiology. I remember trying to help a classmate who had gotten her period: having no idea what that was or what was happening, I only added

---

[127]   Ibid.

to her embarrassment by calling attention to the "mud" all over her chair as I tried to help her. Of course, I had peers who knew much more than I and rumors of dirty secrets were whispered throughout the hallways of our Elementary School, but most of them eluded me.

One dreadful day, however, is forever seared in my memory. Excused from class to use the bathroom, I walked down the empty hallway and swung the heavy door open just enough to slip through. Three girls were clustered against the far wall, their laughter echoing through the cinder block room as they took turns primping in the mirror. As I entered, they turned to study me and asked with sneering smiles, "Are you a virgin?"

I stood silently, staring blankly at them as I puzzled over this unknown word. They repeated the question, following with an insistent, "Yes or no?" The girls leaned in until they were inches from my face. I hesitated and finally blurted out, "I guess so." My eyes scanned their surprised faces as they exchanged looks before erupting in laughter.

"You *guess* so?" they repeated mockingly. "So, you don't *know*?" I pushed past them and slammed the stall door, my face hot with anger. I heard their laughter trail down the hallway as they exited the bathroom.

Tears burned down my face. I hated my innocence, which I blamed for my embarrassment and social immaturity. That incident hardened me: I walked out of the bathroom with steely resolve that I would never find myself in a similar situation. I angrily confronted my mother after school, believing she had deprived me willfully of information I was entitled to. When I asked what a virgin was, the shock on her face

Edward H. Burke found limitations. Burke believed that physiology proved our divinely appointed spheres as women and men. His philosophy limited and defined women according to their reproductive system—its development, monthly cycles, and function in continuing humanity. "[Having a menstrual period] characterizes the female organization, and develops feminine force. Persistence characterizes the male organization, and develops masculine force," he wrote in his 1873 book called *Sex in Education*.[134]

According to Burke, women could essentially not think and menstruate at the same time without compromising one or the other. Educating women in the same subjects as men and allowing them to participate in physical activity would only contribute to her female degeneration, forcing her to become more masculine and stunting her reproductive functions.

Angered, Eliza published a rebuttal called *No Sex in Education: Or, An Equal Chance for Both Boys and Girls* in 1874. Eliza refused to accept Burke's theory, which she claimed "represents woman as normally an invalid for one-fourth of the time."[135] Burke reduced women's unique physiological functions to physical and mental limitations the female body—designed for this purpose—was unable to overcome. But Eliza found the physiological characteristics of women to be naturally equipped with the strength of their function. Her dissertation should echo throughout women's history:

---

[134]   Edward Hammond Clarke, *Sex in Education: Or, A Fair Chance for the Girls* (James R. Osgood and Company, 1873), 120–21.

[135]   Eliza Bisbee Duffey, *No Sex in Education: Or, An Equal Chance for Both Boys and Girls* (J.M. Stoddart & Co., 1874), 18.

"He does not comprehend—he seems never to have realized—the full sense of that which he tries to impress upon his readers, that a woman is not a man in any sense. Accompanying the demand upon her system which nature makes, nature has kindly and wisely—nay, more than that, justly—provided such supplies of strength, vigor and endurance. . . . In his plea for periodicity he does not recognize the fact that there is no periodicity of brain action in a woman. That is ever active and eager, and never calls for periodic rest."[136]

Eliza decried the divisive social education of girls and boys, which allowed boys to be natural, while forcing girls to be artificial. Girls were always kept under high pressure to behave like ladies; forbidden exercise, improperly clothed, stuffed with indigestible food, and only permitted tame recreation. This was "paling their cheeks, dwarfing their physical capabilities, and in their childhood most surely stunting their future womanly development and laying the seeds of life-long disease."[137]

Eliza Bisbee Duffey elevated the role of women and mothers in society, advancing their knowledge and confidence in their physiology and fertility cycles, as well as dispelling the myths of when life begins. She also challenged the virtue of men, writing, "But a masculine weakness is quite as deplorable as a feminine one, and quite as disastrous from an economist's point of view, since, though women must undoubtedly be the mothers of the race, men must be the fathers; and imperfect fatherhood is as great a curse as

---

[136]   Ibid., 24.
[137]   Ibid., 43.

imperfect motherhood, although men, for their own purposes, have not seen fit to so represent it."[138]

The Susan B. Abortion Debate

There is ongoing debate over Susan B. Anthony's position on abortion. Activists on both sides of the "reproductive rights" and "right to life" debate want to claim her as their posthumous representative. As a woman ahead of her time: forward-thinking, quick to act, and outspoken regardless of social consequence, the instances in which Susan B. Anthony referred to abortion categorically clarify her *opposition* to it. Susan poignantly placed abortion with the "monster social evils" emerging from women's "legal subjection to the mastership of a drunken, immoral husband and father."[139] She stated as example: "divorce, adultery, bigamy, seduction, rape . . . scandals and outrages, of wife murders and paramour shooting, of abortions and infanticides,"[140] intentionally listing abortion among the resulting atrocities of alcoholic men forsaking their families.

Susan did not condemn destitute women for resorting to abortion or prostitution, fighting instead against the unjust laws abandoning them to total dependence on seducers or alcoholic and reckless husbands. She was quick to point out in her 1875 *Social Purity* address that prostitutes "constitute but a small portion of the numbers who actually tread the paths of vice and crime . . . continually replenished by

---

[138] Ibid., 54–55.
[139] Ida Husted Harper, *The Life and Work of Susan B. Anthony*, vol. II (Indianapolis: The Bowen-Merrill Co, Indianapolis, 1898), 1004.
[140] Ibid., 1005.

discouraged, seduced, deserted unfortunates, who can no longer hide the terrible secret of their lives."[141]

In addition to those who denied women their dignity and contributed to their fall, Susan abhorred the lack of self-discipline and sacrifice of those women unnecessarily and intentionally choosing abortion over bringing children into the world. On March 4, 1876, a year after her *Social Purity* address, Susan arrived at her brother Daniel's house in Leavenworth, Kansas, and recorded in her diary how her sister-in-law Annie (F. Osborn) was sick in bed for a month due to "tampering with herself" (inducing an abortion). She added, "what ignorance & lack of self-government the world is filled with."[142]

Years later, more public examples of her position appeared in *The Revolution*. Susan and Elizabeth wrote and approved the newspaper's content before publication, refusing to publish advertisements for abortion or contraception. They expressed their opposition to abortion and called for legislative action against advertisements for contraceptives. The April 8, 1869 issue of *The Revolution* applauded the New York legislative bill "for the inspection of all 'patent or quack medicines,'" saying, "It is high time to move for some protection against their deadly influence, moral and spiritual as well as material." The post went on to say that "Restellism has long found in these broths [sic] of Beelzebub, its securest hiding place."[143]

---

141   Ibid.
142   Ann D. Gordon, *The Selected Papers of Elizabeth Cady Stanton & Susan B. Anthony*, vol. 3 (New Brunswick: Rutgers University Press, 2003), 213.
143   *The Revolution*, vol. III, no. 14, New York, Thursday, April 8, 1869, 221.

In the December 2, 1869 edition, under the title "Rest-ellism Exposed," *The Revolution* printed an article commending the female doctor Charlotte Lozier for refusing to perform an abortion, which she called "shameful, revolting, unnatural and unlawful." Having the man requesting the procedure arrested, Dr. Lozier stated that "a person who asks a physician to commit the crime of ante-natal infanticide can be no more considered his patient than one who asks him to poison his wife."[144] *The Revolution* followed with an unquestionably anti-abortion statement: "Some bad women as well as bad men may possibly become doctors, who will do anything for money; but we are sure most women physicians will lend their influence and their aid to shield their sex from the foulest wrong committed against it. It will be a good thing for the community when more women like Mrs. Lozier belong to the profession."[145]

Susan decried that the "holocaust of the womanhood of this nation is sacrificed to the insatiate Moloch of lust" (a Canaanite deity associated in biblical sources with child-sacrifice). Quoting the *Albany Law Journal* of December 1876 on infanticide rates in Washington, DC, she said, "The dead bodies of infants, still-born and murdered, which have been found during the past year, scattered over parks and vacant lots in the city of Washington, are to be numbered by hundreds."[146] Susan cited poverty as the primary cause

---

[144]   *The Revolution*, vol. IV, no. 22, New York, Thursday, December 2, 1869, 346.

[145]   Ibid.

[146]   Ida Husted Harper, *The Life and Work of Susan B. Anthony*, vol. II (Indianapolis: The Bowen-Merrill Co, Indianapolis, 1898), 1005.

of prostitution and abortion, demanding that the law free women from their bondage of dependence upon men.

Susan was compassionate to mothers sacrificing their children to abortion or abandonment for fear of public shame. She shared the alarming statistics of a Catholic Foundling Hospital, which had opened in New York City in 1869, that reported thirteen hundred newborn babies dropped at its door in the hospital's first six months. "That meant thirteen hundred of the daughters of New York, with trembling hands and breaking hearts, trying to bury their sorrow and their shame from the world's cruel gaze. That meant thirteen hundred mothers' hopes blighted and blasted. Thirteen hundred Rachels weeping for their children because they were not!"[147] she commented.

Susan called women to action, stating in her 1875 address, "The work of woman is not to lessen the severity or the certainty of the penalty for the violation of the moral law, but to prevent this violation by the removal of the causes which lead to it."[148] In the spirit of Susan B. Anthony's teaching, the work of women would be to establish foundling hospitals to shelter those infants who would otherwise be in danger, to pass laws empowering women in tough situations to create a new life for themselves and their children, and to build greater virtue within male and female children so that they would not be slaves to their natural passions.

---

[147]   Ibid.
[148]   Ibid., 1006.

PART TWO

Voluntary Motherhood

A New Era of Feminism
– Twentieth Century

*"Who was that dainty feminist who informed the public that
as soon as women got the vote, they would make the laws
for working women and children?—How hopeful!"*[149]

—*The Woman Rebel*, 1914

By the turn of the century, the suffrage movement had established momentum with a future. It had grown twenty thousand times in size from the initial one hundred Declaration signatures gained at the first Woman's Rights Convention in Seneca Falls in 1848. Midwesterner Carrie Chapman Catt assumed leadership of the American Woman Suffrage Association (NAWSA) from Susan B. Anthony in 1900 and worked hard to make its membership soar to two million. The NAWSA became the League of Women Voters, which is still active today, by the time of the ratification of the Nineteenth Amendment in 1920.

The first half of the twentieth century brought both evolution and division to the women's movement. Radical suffragette Alice Paul broke with the NAWSA and began the

---

[149] *The Woman Rebel*, vol. I, no. 1, March 1914, 3.

Woman's Party in 1916, following the model of England's militant women's campaign. Paul led protests challenging President Woodrow Wilson and was repeatedly arrested. Black women fought their own battle for suffrage, largely left out of the women's movement, and even requested to march at the back of the Woman Suffrage Procession in 1913. They formed the National Association of Colored Women in 1896, which organized to help African-American women gain suffrage, civil rights, and overcome injustice. The Civil Rights Act of 1964, which ended segregation policies in the United States, helped black women to continue to gain momentum in their fight for equal rights.

The women's movement had expanded from one primarily focused on suffrage to advocating for women's equal rights as they entered the workplace in greater numbers and began demanding reproductive freedom through contraception and abortion rights. In this new age of feminism, which had transmuted from its original endeavor, the movement needed philosophical clarity and structure to unify the momentum that was building.

Margaret Sanger became a key player in the pivotal fight to introduce and promote birth control methods in America, which wildly changed its sexual landscape. Through her radical publications, birth control clinics, and establishment of Planned Parenthood, Sanger challenged the Catholic Church, society, and the structure of the American family. Beyond her efforts, feminist philosophy in the twentieth century was largely formed around two seminal works: Simone de Beauvoir's *The Second Sex*, which determined femininity to be a social construct, and Betty Friedan's *The*

Feminine Mystique, which purported to unveil the misery of the American housewife. Both gave new voice to the female condition in America and greatly influenced feminist ideology. The term "feminism" was embraced through books and magazines, ushering in its second wave.

Taking aim at social and cultural inequalities, the movement encouraged women to break free from the "shackles" of domesticity and motherhood. Through the Industrial Revolutions, civil rights movements, and women's participation in World War II, feminists demanded economic and social justice, and sought to undermine American patriarchy and deconstruct traditional gender roles. The demand for "voluntary motherhood" became a feminist battle cry. As Margaret Sanger wrote in her 1938 autobiography, "I knew something must be done to rescue those women who were voiceless; someone had to express with white hot intensity the conviction that they must be empowered to decide for themselves when they should fulfill the supreme function of motherhood. They had to be made aware of how they were being shackled, and roused to mutiny."[150]

Teenage Angst

"How great a forest is set ablaze by a small fire!"[151]

Sometime in my early adolescence, my parents went to Puerto Rico and left my brother and me in the care of our grandparents. I had been working for several days on

---

[150] Margaret Sanger, *The Autobiography of Margaret Sanger* (Stellar Classics, 2017), 106.

[151] James 3:5.

building a hot air balloon, which I believed could be powered with a hairdryer. I decided to test the wind's ability to carry it from a high height and lumbered up to the roof of our home, dragging it behind. Thankfully, my brother, possessing far more sense than I did, ran to get my frazzled grandparents, who swore they would never watch us again.

Being the artistic melodramatic in the family became increasingly challenging through the years. As a child, everyone got a good laugh out of my living room productions, backyard Olympic games, and magic shows in which I made my brother disappear. But as I got older, my artistic loves became clearly defined as a frivolous pastime. I embraced the literary characters in books over actual children my age and concerned myself more with imagination than with the changing relationships between boys and girls happening all around me.

My peers were consumed with the cyclical art of flirtation, which inevitably seemed to be followed by the despair of rejection. They were poisonously entangled in self-deprecating gossip and manipulation. The media encouraged these dark social arts, which made us think that girls our age *should* be concerned with these frivolous things. I watched friends form obsessions with their outward appearances as vanity masqueraded as a virtue. The messages of commercials and teen magazines were turning our fragile egos into envy. We were splashed by media with weight loss ads, tips to make our appearances better, countless sob stories of girls struggling with their identity, and instructions on how to become more pleasing to boys. For the first time, I became self-conscious about my body. I mourned over my dark almond-shaped eyes after reading that the perfect eye-shape was round. I flipped desperately through the magazine pages to find the few girls with dark eyes and hair like mine, only to realize that they were also depressingly flawless. It became painfully clear to me that a woman's outward beauty was truly her greatest virtue.

I listened carefully to the wounded lyrics of the grunge songs haunting the radio, realizing that *nobody* was truly happy and that there was ultimately no point to life. Discovering this both stifled and depressed me. The joy went out of life as I stopped singing, dancing, and even outwardly expressing myself. I became consumed by the hopeless grunge lyrics and hid my creative heart in my artwork and the words I entrusted to my notebooks. I had lost my carefree childhood and struggled with a necessary detachment from my outward appearance.

But the most devastating loss of those years was the loss of my religion. Possessing a poor understanding of Christianity and a lack of hope as I approached the age of teenage angst proved detrimental. My brother and I began to resist going to Mass and spiritual formation with every negative and lethargic word or action we could muster. I could find no rhyme or reason to Catholic spirituality, and I was tired of being forced to follow empty and dated traditions.

My parents eventually gave in to our demands. Despite their best efforts to give us a faith foundation, they also lacked the spiritual arsenal of truth to win our weak battle. Our family discontinued any further spiritual formation and no longer upheld our Sunday obligation to attend Mass. In reversing the scriptural promise of the house of Joshua, our family's spiritual motto became, "As for me and my house, we will *not* serve the Lord." Our family was spiritually unguarded and unprotected, and all spiritual doors were being opened.

I should have been ecstatic over my defeat, but I wasn't. Although it seemed inconsequential at first, life without faith began to feel unnatural. I couldn't understand how burning incense and the repetitive recitation of scripted prayers could possibly save my soul. I wouldn't know for many years afterward what a spiritual deprivation the loss of my religion ultimately was.

The Riot Grrrl

High School felt like a strange coming-of-age drama being performed on a small stage cast with emotional adolescents. We were each grappling with our part in the play. The angry dark lyrics of the '90s grunge songs were our soundtrack and their twisted outlooks on life had become our religion. The fragments of morality from my catechetical youth seemed to be remnants of a hypocritical religion. My Catholic faith was scattered among relativism.

I spent most of my days in our high school's art studio by the time I was a senior. I had four elective art classes and was on track to gain acceptance to an art school after graduation. My high school career had largely been spent among other artists and musicians. We were the misfit outcasts in our high school's microcosm of the real world. That was the role we had chosen.

I entered freshman year searching for a purpose and desiring rebellion. I met the girl who opened wide that door to me shortly after. It was the metaphorical door to becoming a part of something greater than myself, which I had struggled to find. Her name was Jolene and she was a self-proclaimed "feminist." I had never met a feminist before meeting Jolene, and she was exciting and dangerous. She possessed an unconventional mystery and the promise of a new adventure, which my heart craved.

Jolene's short bleached blonde hair was holding onto the remnants of a faded pink dye. She wore a tight tee-shirt with a band logo atop checkered skater pants. One of her belt loops was securing a chain connected to the wallet in her pocket, and a small silver stud sparkled from the piercing in the side of her nose. Nothing about Jolene conformed to any norm. She seemed to master the best of masculinity and femininity all in her tiny force of a being.

I was instantly captivated by Jolene's unique and flippant attitude toward conformity. She was miles apart from our peers, who were desperately struggling to fit in. Her carefree attitude also wielded a fierce strength when she felt threatened. Jolene's presence commanded respect, even from the most judgmental students. I was fascinated by the way that she outwardly manifested the nonconforming identity most of us owned in the secrecy of our thoughts.

Jolene found a kindred spirit in me, and she took me under her broken wing. We spent countless hours together as my interest grew in the political women's issues she was passionate about. She shared personal instances of abuse from her past, and I despised the wrongs committed against her. We spoke of the injustices women had suffered throughout history and continued to suffer. I was haunted by the literary characters of Mary Wollstonecraft's *Maria*, Virginia Woolf's *A Room of One's Own*, and Sylvia Plath's *The Bell Jar*. Those well-constructed feminine characters who had been subjected to an unjust fate had come alive. I discovered that my purpose was also to take a place in liberating women further.

Jolene introduced me to the underground feminist punk movement known as the "riot grrrl" movement. Often associated with third-wave feminism, the riot grrrl movement combined punk music with feminist consciousness and politics. It boldly confronted the heavy moral topics of lesbianism, bipolar depression, sexism, and rape. The riot grrrl movement also produced female bands who unleashed a proactive feminist message layered on top of the forceful punk sound I loved. I found in it the perfect comingling of feminism and music.

I quickly replaced my music collection of the mournful men of grunge with the fierce and energetic punk women preaching anti-fashion and female empowerment. Discovering the riot grrrl movement was my coming-of-age moment, my enlightenment. I memorized the abrasive monologues of female bands such as *Bikini Kill*, which I played endlessly on repeat. I subscribed to the thriving underground press of the punk (maga) "zine" subculture and rejected conventional American politics and religion. I espoused radical ideas of communism, socialism, and anarchy, and I protested the injustices plaguing many disenfranchised people, especially women.

Freeing my repressed artistic soul to join forces with the riot grrrl movement bore in me a hot-headed feminist-seeking restitution. Scripture tells us, "The eye is the lamp of the body," and mine were covered in layers of black eyeliner and filled with darkness. I adopted the eclectic riot grrrl fashion style, which rejected conventional norms of fashion and hailed personal freedom of expression. Being "feminine" was independently interpreted, and we often defied society's traditional feminine attributes. All of our actions were intended to make a statement. Some riot grrrl activists wore little to no clothing on stage, while violently yelling lyrics opposed to sexism and assault. These contradictory messages often convoluted the statement being made.

It was daunting to radically change my appearance in high school, which won me the senior superlative of "most changed." I hated being gawked at and treated differently by others for my appearance, but I also couldn't stand blending into the crowd. I quickly realized that I couldn't wear purple fishnet stockings and green converse or spray-painted doc martens without changing everything else in my life to match. A knit cap covered my head at our family dinner table, regardless of the season, in order to avoid an explosive battle over the colorful hair it was concealing. I attended parties and snuck out of the house regularly, experimenting with every freedom under the sun. Most of my friends' parents did drugs and didn't care what we did, which made me feel even more stifled by my strict parents. My untrustworthy and disobedient behavior at home caused constant contention between my parents and me, which, in my view, was a further confirmation of their shallow love for me.

As the riot grrrl movement of feminism continued to encourage me to tackle issues of morality, repression, and social expression, I repetitively encountered the issues of reproductive rights—abortion, contraception, and fertility. During that time, the horror of being a woman was awakened in me. I felt defenseless against social repression and sexual assault and against years of unending childbirth and involuntary motherhood. The awareness of my fertility was crippling and seemed inescapable. I made the clear decision to never marry or become a mother and to protect those women who needed the defense of the feminist revolution. No person and no law would intrude upon our freedom.

Margaret Sanger and Birth Control

"Perhaps it would be as well to explain how I came to take an interest in the question of birth control. For fourteen years I worked as a trained nurse in the slum areas of New York City. I came in daily contact with the terrific human waste of children and of mothers—children who died before they were a year old, 90 per cent. Through poverty and neglect, and mothers who died from causes due to ignorant maternity."[152]

—Margaret Sanger, "Women Enslaved by Maternity," 1920

On the morning of October 16, 1916, Margaret Sanger, her sister Ethel, and friend Fania opened the doors of the very first birth control clinic in America. It was a revolutionary moment in American history, forever reshaping feminism, sexuality, and motherhood. The clinic served impoverished women in the Brownsville Section of Brooklyn, "bursting with excess of wretched humanity." It was Margaret's laborious "child" of years of unrelenting contraceptive research and nursing experience, which promised at last to protect mothers from the physical and financial detriment of excessive childbearing. The three pioneers of reproductive

---

[152]   Margaret Sanger, "Women Enslaved by Maternity," *Lloyd's Sunday News*, May 16, 1920.

rights stopped at the local drugstore and "arranged with the proprietor to prepare himself for supplying the pessiaries we were going to recommend" before opening the doors to 150 women on their first day. However, the clinic lasted only two weeks before being shut down as a "public nuisance."

It's hard to believe that there was ever a time in this country when doctors didn't hand out birth control like candy, much less allow citizens to openly explore the topic. I remember my mother taking me to our general practitioner around the age of sixteen. I had been wrestling with depression and such painful and heavy periods that I usually missed school on the first day of each cycle, spending the day in bed cursing my sex. After ten minutes of explaining my erratic premenstrual moods and crippling physical symptoms to a physician I had never met, she quickly scratched out two prescriptions for an anti-depressant and birth control, enthusiastically adding how it would also clear my acne. With that, she walked out, leaving in my very incapable teenage hands two prescriptions possessing the power to greatly alter my life. Shrugging and believing that "doctor knows best," Mom and I headed to the pharmacy to fill the prescriptions.

I knew nothing of the detrimental effects of ingesting a type-1 carcinogen or how the smartly packaged pills of synthetic estrogen and progesterone would wreak havoc on my already unstable emotions. Worse, the pills suppressed my alarming symptoms with an undesired band-aid effect. Before long I discovered in the worst of ways that the pill's side effects were oddly less desirable than the disease itself. Disposing of them, I settled hopelessly to relying on the anti-depressants to carry me through the remaining forty-odd years of fertility.

Was sixteen too early for a hysterectomy? Knowing that I never wanted children and that over half of American women were using some form of contraception,[153] I found it status quo, and even posh, to be among that number. The daunting years of possible childbearing ahead seemed unfair. After all, Margaret Sanger had offered her life's work for the cause of bringing contraception to American women, and we had the right to use it!

The Socialist Seed

This misguided and distorted sentiment, expressed by my teenage-self, was why Margaret Sanger became a hero to many. She *was* the social rights pioneer who dedicated most of her life to fixing the unsolvable problem of involuntary motherhood and setting women *free* from becoming "a child-bearing machine." Born in south central New York to Irish parents, Margaret Higgins was the sixth of eleven children. Her father was a Socialist, and his freethinking philosophies heavily influenced her, while at the same time branding her and her siblings in the eyes of their community as "children of the devil." Deploring the Catholic dogma of his upbringing, her father contributed to Margaret's belief that "[socialist] ideals still come nearest to carrying out what Christianity was supposed to do."[154] She reflected in

---

[153]   Centers for Disease Control and Prevention, *Current Contraceptive Status Among Women Aged 15-49: United States, 2015-2017.*
[154]   Margaret Sanger, *The Autobiography of Margaret Sanger* (Stellar Classics, 2017), 23.

her autobiography that her parents' unusual comradeship of love and respect allowed them to live happily the life of an artist's family—"chickens today and feathers tomorrow."

Margaret described her childhood as poor but relatively happy, only interrupted by the despair of her four-year-old brother's death from croup. She underwent the traumatic experience of unearthing his coffin and working for days to make a memorial death mask of him with her father. Margaret also recalled that despite her father's great affection for her mother, he hopelessly disappointed her in his guardianship of their home, saying that his "liberal views were so well known that our house was marked."[155] One winter, her father's open-door policy nearly killed her mother as two strangers raided their home and left her unconscious in the cold. Her mother's poor health worsened due to the ensuing pneumonia, which ultimately contributed to her death by pulmonary tuberculosis.

Margaret took an interest in women's rights early in her education and rebelled against the idea that matrimony was a woman's only future option. Reflecting on the families of her hometown, she made the everlasting assessment that "large families were associated with poverty, toil, unemployment, drunkenness, cruelty, fighting, jails; the small ones with cleanliness, leisure, freedom, light, space, sunshine." This assessment planted a seed in Margaret Sanger's heart that grew into a monstrous forest. She wrote in her 1938 autobiography, "To me the distinction between happiness

---

[155]   Ibid., 32.

and unhappiness in childhood was one of small families and of large families rather than of wealth and poverty."[156]

Margaret's hospice care for her mother resulted in her own development of tubercular glands, but it also awakened her desire to study medicine. She pursued nursing and assisted on many maternity cases where she was both overcome by the beauty of birth and also deeply affected by the "pathetically, plaintively, hopefully" pleading patients, desperate to avoid another successive conception. Margaret wrote, "To see a baby born is one of the greatest experiences that a human being can have. Birth to me has always been more awe-inspiring than death. As often as I have witnessed the miracle, held the perfect creature with its tiny hands and tiny feet, each time I have felt as though I were entering a cathedral with prayer in my heart."[157]

Not able to justify pushing aside the women desperate to avoid successive pregnancies, Margaret ruminated this question as she encountered her own motherhood. She married an architect named William Sanger in 1902 and experienced a miserable first pregnancy the following year. Due to her illness, Margaret awaited childbirth in the "gloomy environment" of a semi-sanitarium while undergoing treatment by a pulmonary tuberculosis specialist. She lived the following eight months of postpartum in an Adirondack village with baby Stuart and a nurse who was recommended for her recovery. As her health worsened, Margaret recalled, "I was not even interested in my baby."[158]

---

[156]   Ibid., 28.
[157]   Ibid., 55.
[158]   Ibid., 60.

When Margaret and baby Stuart were finally able to return home for the remainder of her recovery, the Sangers decided to join a suburban colony in Westchester. After rebuilding their home, which had been destroyed by fire, Margaret gave birth to their second son, Grant. "I loved having a baby to tend again, and wanted at least four more as quickly as my health would permit," the birth control advocate confessed in her autobiography.[159] Margaret realized this desire again, just twenty months later, when she delivered her daughter Peggy. Her illness again cropped up after Peggy's birth, and "the doctor said my family must end at this point."[160]

The Sangers quickly grew discontent with "tame domesticity" and were led by their longings for wider horizons to an apartment in uptown New York. Margaret recalled, "A religion without a name was spreading over the country. The converts were liberals, Socialists, anarchists, revolutionists of all shades. . . . Our living room became a gathering place where liberals, anarchists, Socialists, and I.W.W.'s could meet."[161] Finding that her "own personal feelings drew [her] towards the individualistic, anarchist philosophy, . . . it seemed to [her] necessary to approach the ideal by way of Socialism."[162] Margaret joined the Socialist Party, which became a door into the radical world of New York's underground political activists. She was quickly selected to recruit new members of working women to the Socialist Party, which she said was "proof that we were not necessarily like

---

[159]   Ibid., 65.
[160]   Ibid., 65.
[161]   Ibid., 70.
[162]   Ibid., 75.

the masculine, aggressive, bulldog, window-smashing suffragettes in England."[163]

The Tipping Point

In 1911, Margaret began publishing articles discussing health topics in the Socialist newspaper the *New York Call*. Her series, *What Every Mother Should Know*, followed by *What Every Girl Should Know*, were so popular that they attracted the inevitable attention of the Comstock Law. In retaliation to threats of revoking their mailing privileges, the *Call* released a large box under its usual section for *What Every Girl Should Know* containing the words: NOTHING! "By Order of the Post-Office Department." The public backlash of reader complaints due to the censorship of Margaret's article was momentous in challenging the federal obscenity laws and in proving the public's desire for sex education.

Margaret shifted her focus to a new social revolution, which targeted the maternity concerns of the poor. She said, "I always came back to the idea which was beginning to obsess me—that something more was needed to assuage the condition of the very poor."[164] As her nursing duties called her more frequently to maternity cases on New York's Lower East Side, she felt "the utmost depression" toward the desperate circumstances of its impoverished mothers, as well as her utter helplessness in offering any hope of protection from their burden of constant childbearing.

---

[163]   Ibid.
[164]   Ibid., 85.

Margaret recalled, "Pregnancy was a chronic condition among women of this class," telling how they passed contraceptive and abortion remedies among them of "herb teas, turpentine, steaming, rolling downstairs, inserting slippery elm, knitting needles, shoe-hooks." She went on to say, "On Saturday nights I have seen groups of from fifty to one hundred with their shawls over their heads waiting outside the office of a five-dollar abortionist."[165] Margaret never felt at ease among these poor mothers and was desperate to find a preventative cure to their perpetual childbearing. "I hated the wretchedness and hopelessness of the poor, and never experienced that satisfaction in working among them that so many noble women have found," she confessed in her autobiography.[166]

Margaret finally reached her tipping point in mid-July 1912 when she attended to a twenty-eight-year-old patient. Mrs. Sachs had been found by her husband unconscious on the floor and surrounded by their three young children. She was suffering from the results of a self-induced abortion, and Margaret and the doctor fought the patient's septicemia for three weeks until they were confident of her survival. Margaret reported that the doctor warned the patient that another pregnancy would kill her. However, when Mrs. Sachs inquired *how* to prevent another pregnancy, the doctor only scoffed, responding, "You want to have your cake and eat it too, do you? Well, it can't be done."[167]

---

165   Ibid., 89.
166   Ibid., 86–87.
167   Ibid., 91.

Margaret was moved to despair as the young patient begged her for answers, and she promised to somehow provide them on her next visit. For three months, Margaret avoided her promise, although she was continuously haunted by the "Madonna-like expression" of Mrs. Sachs. Not long after, Mr. Sachs called once again with the dreaded news that "his wife was sick again and from the same cause."[168] By the time Margaret arrived at their home, Mrs. Sachs had slipped into a coma; she died ten minutes later.

A restless night consumed Margaret after leaving the home of the distraught husband and children of Mrs. Sachs. She recounted in her autobiography the unbearable pictures in her mind of women writhing in the pain of childbirth, babies wrapped in newspapers, starving children in rags, and an endless succession of death and coffins. Margaret said definitively that night, "I went to bed, knowing that no matter what it might cost, I was finished with palliatives and superficial cures; I was resolved to seek out the root of evil, to do something to change the destiny of mothers whose miseries were vast as the sky."[169]

After the death of Mrs. Sachs, Margaret renounced nursing and dedicated her time to discovering "a simple method of contraception for the poor."[170] The Sangers moved to France in 1913, allowing Margaret to search Europe for contraceptive answers and to study "the conditions resulting from generations of family limitation."[171] The radical French

---

[168]   Ibid.
[169]   Ibid., 92.
[170]   Ibid., 94.
[171]   Ibid., 96.

syndicalists of the labor movement were promoting the practice of "conscious generation," which incorporated what she said was the "perfect acceptance of family limitation and its relation to labor."[172] Most French women only had one or two children because they were taught how to regulate their fertility with homemade suppositories before marriage and frequented abortionists after.

Margaret had compiled enough contraceptive information by the end of the year to leave France and begin working on her ground-breaking American publication. But her work had taken precedence over her marriage, which she admitted "had not failed because of lack of love, romance, wealth, respect . . . but because the interests of each had widened beyond those of the other."[173] Margaret left her husband in France in December 1913 and returned to New York alone with the children.

The Woman Rebel

Margaret Sanger returned to New York ignited with the fervor to start a new movement, which, she said, "had much more to it than just the prevention of conception."[174] As she formed a society, Margaret struggled over its name. Favoring the word "control" in the new society's title, Margaret considered "population control, race control, and birth rate control" before settling on the lasting term: "birth control." *The National Birth Control League* officially took form in

---

[172]   Ibid., 104.
[173]   Ibid., 136.
[174]   Ibid., 108.

1914 and began releasing a radical monthly newspaper, stating, "It will be the aim of the WOMAN REBEL to advocate the prevention of conception and to impart such knowledge in the columns of this paper. Other subjects, including slavery through motherhood; through things, the home, public opinion and so forth."[175] Receiving no support from feminists, Margaret turned to the Socialists and trade unionists. The first issue of the *Woman Rebel* was published in March 1914 under the slogan "No Gods, No Masters."

As the *Woman Rebel* fought continuous legal battles over its rights of distribution, Margaret returned to what she considered her most urgent and primary purpose: the production and distribution of a pamphlet called *Family Limitation*. She compiled all the French contraceptive material she had collected, and when threatened with a potential forty-five-year prison sentence by a pending indictment for the *Woman Rebel*, she rushed the pamphlet's progress.

Finding a linotype operator willing to print one hundred thousand copies of the pamphlet after hours, Margaret secretly sent them to contacts across the United States. She then made permanent arrangements for the care of her children as she fled to Canada and then to England the night before her trial. Margaret wrote, "Parting from all that I held dear in life, I left New York at midnight, without a passport, not knowing whether I could ever return."[176] She boarded the *RMS Virginian* under the name Bertha Watson. Three days out of Montreal, Margaret sent a cable to her US

---

[175] *The Woman Rebel*, vol. I, no. 1, March 1914.
[176] Sanger, *The Autobiography of Margaret Sanger*, 120.

contacts signaling the simultaneous national release of *Family Limitation* as she sailed to her escape.

Family Limitation quickly spread across America, making Margaret Sanger a household name. Meanwhile, in England, Margaret prepared "to make [her] trial soundly historical so that birth control would be seriously discussed in America," she wrote in 1938.[177] Spending hours in research at the British Museum, Margaret connected the history of contraceptive theorists, beginning with Malthus, who was considered the father of family limitation. She agreed with Malthus on the need for population control, which was believed to be outweighing the global food supply. But the only solution Malthus offered in the eighteenth century was later marriages built upon financial stability. A century later, Francis Place, in his 1822 *Proofs of the Principle of Population,* criticized Malthus for insinuating that the poor have no right to eat when unemployed and for shrinking "from discussing the propriety of preventing conception."[178] John Stuart Mill argued in his 1826 publication of the *Elements of Political Economy* that "either marriages are sparingly contracted, or care is taken that children, beyond a certain number, shall not be the fruit."[179]

Margaret followed further down the overpopulation rabbit hole to Robert Dale Owen's *Moral Physiology.* Owen's 1841 book boasted a utilitarian quote on its title page and

---

[177] Ibid., 125.

[178] Francis Place, *Illustrations and Proofs of the Principle of Population* (London: 1822), 173.

[179] John Stuart Mill, *Elements of Political Economy*, (London, 1826), 50.

was hailed by Madame Restell's husband, Charles Lohman. His divorce legislation had also influenced Elizabeth Cady Stanton. Owen's *Moral Physiology* offered a mode of preventing conception by "complete withdrawal, on the part of the man, immediately previous to emission."[180] Owen declared his withdrawal method to be morally "an act of practical virtue."[181] American physician and atheist, Dr. Charles Knowlton then wrote his *Fruits of Philosophy* in 1879, which openly recommended a chemical formula for "destroying the fecundating property of the sperm."[182]

Charles Knowlton was the advocate for chemical contraception whom Margaret had been searching for. Knowlton was a medical doctor seeking a way "whereby men and women may refrain at will from becoming parents, without even a partial sacrifice of the pleasure which attends the gratification of their productive instinct."[183] He argued that contraceptive methods were a "great utility . . . especially for the poor." Knowlton declared it "the duty of the physician to inform mankind of the means of preventing the evils that are liable to arise from gratifying the reproductive instinct."[184]

Inspired by her research, Margaret befriended the British Neo-Malthusian Society, who boasted the only remedy to cure society's disease. She remarked of the society in her autobiography: "Instead of the impractical advice of Malthus to marry late, the Neo-Malthusians advised early marriage,

---

[180]   Robert Dale Owen, *Moral Physiology*, (London, 1841), 36.
[181]   Ibid., 39.
[182]   Charles Knowlton, *Fruits of Philosophy* (Rotterdam, 1878), 73.
[183]   Ibid., iii.
[184]   Ibid., 11.

the use of contraceptive methods, and children born according to the earning capacity of the father."[185] The society's influential leaders taught Margaret their tactic of educating the educators and influencing the social influencers, holding the belief that the lower classes would follow.

Her final stop was the Netherlands, where its first female physician, Dr. Aletta Jacobs, was giving contraceptive advice in her clinics. According to Margaret, the Netherlands were the "force operating towards constructive race building," and the Dutch attitude of "looking upon having a baby as an economic luxury" contributed immensely to their low maternal and infant death rate. Due to their proper spacing of children, the Netherlands also had the most rapidly increasing population in Europe, but according to Margaret, "not too rapid to permit those already born to be assured of livelihood."[186] The model of personal instruction given in the Netherland clinics was a game changer for Margaret, who concluded that "clinics were the proper places for which to disseminate information."[187]

The First Clinic

"I had a vision of a "chain"—thousands of them in every center of America, staffed with specialists putting the subject on a modern scientific basis through research," she recorded of her future birth control clinics.[188] At the start of World War I in 1914, Bill Sanger was sent back to New York from

---

[185]   Sanger, *The Autobiography of Margaret Sanger*, 128.
[186]   Ibid., 146.
[187]   Ibid., 152.
[188]   Ibid., 190.

France. Visited at his studio by a man pleading for a copy of *Family Limitation*, Bill ironically gave the man his only copy. Days later, Bill was arrested for circulating obscene literature by Anthony Comstock. His trial and thirty-day jail sentence were the catalysts precipitating Margaret's return to New York to face her own fight.

Margaret sailed from France, initially intending to gather her children and sneak back across the ocean. In New York, however, she discovered that the National Birth Control League had reorganized in her absence and was now denying her both sanction and support. The Academy of Medicine also denied her their support. In the wake of these disappointing social and political abandonments, Margaret faced the deeper tragedy of losing her five-year-old daughter Peggy to pneumonia on November 6, 1915, just days after she arrived home. Margaret lamented, "The joy in the fullness of life went out of it then and has never quite returned."[189]

Due to the overwhelming outpouring of public sentiment in the wake of her loss, Margaret was released from her federal indictment. The press also rallied behind her to influence even the Birth Control League to realign publicly with her. Encouraged by the public momentum, Margaret left her "Birth Control" office on Fifth Avenue in the spring of 1916 for a national lecture tour. She organized her talking points into "seven circumstances under which birth control should be practiced." These included parents with transmissible diseases such as epilepsy, insanity, or syphilis; parents with a temporary condition of the lungs, heart, or kidneys;

---

[189]   Ibid., 182.

parents having produced other subnormal children; adolescent parents (twenty-two years or younger for the wife and twenty-three years or younger for the husband); and what she deemed as an inadequate earning capacity of the father; as well as a mother who had given birth within the last two to three years. Margaret stated in her lectures, "Every young couple should practice birth control for at least one year after marriage and two as a rule."[190]

She recalled being shocked on her lecture tour to discover that "anyone, no matter how ignorant, how diseased mentally or physically, how lacking in all knowledge of children, seemed to consider he or she had the right to become a parent."[191] Margaret began employing the Neo-Malthusian tactic of influencing the influencers. She gave a significant speech at the National Social Workers' Conference in Indianapolis, scolding the social workers for their temporary accomplishments and useless efforts of charity. Margaret said, "They could never attain their ideal of eliminating the problems of the masses until the breeding of the unending stream of unwanted babies was stopped."[192] She considered that speech to be a home run, recalling that "the social agents, like the plumed darts of a seeded dandelion puffed into the air, scattered to every quarter of the country; thereafter, to the West and back again, I heard echoes of the meeting."[193]

Margaret returned to New York from her lecture tour to realize her dream of opening the nation's first birth control

---

190   Ibid., 193–94.
191   Ibid., 195.
192   Ibid., 198–99.
193   Ibid., 199.

clinic in Brooklyn on October 16, 1916. Modeled after the Netherlands clinics, Margaret said, "We explained simply what contraception was; that abortion was the wrong way— no matter how early it was performed it was taking life; that contraception was the better way, the safer way."[194] The police forced eviction papers and arrested Margaret, her sister Ethel, and their friend Fania, finding all three guilty and sentencing Margaret and Ethel to thirty days in the Workhouse on Blackwell Island.

Ethel's front-page hunger strike caused Margaret to be sent to Queens County Penitentiary in Long Island. There, her active tuberculosis granted her a special diet and pardon from work, including cleaning her cell. Margaret devoted her time to research and made a study of the incarcerated women based on their family size.

---

[194]   Ibid., 217.

The Spearhead

*"I told them . . . my private and personal conception of
what Feminism should mean; that is, women should
first free themselves from biological slavery, which could
best be accomplished through birth control."[195]*

—Margaret Sanger, Autobiography

Prison didn't stop Margaret from affecting the public.
In February 1917, while she was still in the penitentiary, her first issue of the *Birth Control Review* was released.
Margaret noted that this publication of the birth control
movement, "from 1917 to 1921, was the spearhead in the
educational stage."[196] She released a birth control documentary after completing her jail sentence, but the movement's
progress was temporarily halted due to World War I. Still,
Margaret celebrated her "section on venereal disease in *What
Every Girl Should Know* . . . reprinted and distributed among
the soldiers going into cantonments and abroad."[197]

She opposed the many Americans turning to religion
during the time of war, stating that "with every act I was

---

[195] Ibid., 171.
[196] Ibid., 252.
[197] Ibid., 256.

progressing in accord with a universal law of evolution—
moral evolution."[198] She recited a biblical verse from Sirach
when encountering Christian opposition to the birth control movement, which read, "Do not desire a multitude of
useless children." The following line, however, which Margaret failed to include, reads, "nor rejoice in ungodly sons, If
they multiply, do not rejoice in them, unless the fear of the
Lord is in them."[199]■

Margaret never disguised her disdain for the Catholic
clergy. She cynically calculated the beneficiary cost of large
families to the Church in baptismal fees, baby funerals,
Masses, and candles for the repose of baby souls, and the
emotional torment of parents, asking, "Is this the price of
Christianity?" Margaret verbally attacked a young priest
opposing her contraceptive bill in Connecticut in 1921, asking, "Why, above all, was he celibate, thus outraging nature's
primary demand on the human species—to propagate its
kind."[200] She was shocked when visiting Ireland in 1920 to
hear priests speaking *against* overly large families and grew
hopeful that birth control might also solve the Church's
problems. She recorded in her autobiography that "it would
be better for the Catholic Church as well as for the world if
they could help people to have only a few children and bring
them up decently."[201]

Margaret published *Woman and the New Race* in 1920,
followed by giving a series of lectures in England for the

---

[198]   Ibid., 260.
[199]   Sirach 16:2.
[200]   Sanger, *The Autobiography of Margaret Sanger*, 294.
[201]   Ibid., 278.

Neo-Malthusian League. There she encountered Socialist and Marxist opposition, fearing that birth control and "any reform likely to dull the edge of poverty was bad for Socialism because it made labor less dissatisfied."[202] But Margaret remained focused on her European goal to discover a means of chemical contraception, which was "cheap, harmless, easily applied." She went to Germany, but found 1920s Germany to be a horrific site, recounting that "working women had been forced down to a state beside the lower animals. . . . I heard countless stories from mothers who had been tortured by watching their children slowly starve to death."[203]

The German Neo-Malthusians were demanding the right to abortion. Berlin's statistics proved that "out of forty-thousand known pregnancies twenty-three thousand were terminated by this means, though it was technically illegal."[204] The German medical solution was evidenced by a medical professional Margaret interviewed, who said, "By aborting the mothers, we are doing our best to cope with conditions as we find them."[205] Another German gynecologist told her, "We will never give over the control of our numbers to the women themselves. . . . With abortions it is in our hands; we make the decisions, and they must come to us."[206] Margaret was appalled by the practice of abortion, which she found to be "a ridiculous substitute for contraceptives."[207] Her concern was "to prevent entrance into the

---

[202]   Ibid., 275.
[203]   Ibid., 282.
[204]   Ibid., 285.
[205]   Ibid.
[206]   Ibid., 286.
[207]   Ibid.

world of those children whose backs were so weak that they could never sit up straight, whose bones were too soft to hold the weight of their bodies."[208]

She arrived in Munich at the height of the "birth strike," which resulted from the Communist dissemination of contraceptive information throughout Bavaria. There Margaret was finally able to track down the chemist responsible for making an innovative contraceptive jelly. Together they established an international partnership, and Margaret "inaugurated a new phase in the movement—the use of a chemical contraceptive."[209]

Human Laboratory

The year 1921 was laden with enormously significant birth control events. Margaret Sanger began pushing a bill through the New York legislature to legally expand the use of contraceptives. At the same time, she began a clinic on East Tenth Street, which was intended as "a nucleus for research on scientific methods of contraception." The clinic offered a day nursery, weekly sessions on prenatal care and marital adjustment, a gynecologist, a sterility specialist, a psychiatrist, and a eugenics consultant. Margaret recorded, "Since the hospitals were laggard in this matter, I decided to open a second clinic of my own. It was to be in effect a laboratory dealing in human beings instead of mice. . . . I was going to suggest to women that in the Twentieth Century they give

---

[208]   Ibid., 285.
[209]   Ibid., 290.

themselves to science as they had in the past given their lives to religion."[210]

The American Birth Control League was launched to build positive public opinion on birth control as Margaret planned the first National Birth Control Conference to be held at the Plaza Hotel in New York. She subsequently published her book *The Pivot of Civilization* in 1922, claiming that society's central challenge was the control and guidance of sex. In the book, Margaret wrote, "Mastery of this force is possible only through the instrument of Birth Control."[211]

The Birth Control Conference was shut down by Archbishop Patrick J. Hayes, and Margaret was again arrested. She angrily wrote an open letter to Archbishop Hayes, challenging his claim that birth control was "a diabolical thing."[212] The archbishop responded with haunting clarity amid the moral chaos and social upheaval caused by the birth control movement: "To take human life after its inception is a horrible crime; but to prevent human life that the Creator is about to bring into being is satanic. In the first instance, the body is killed, while the soul lives on; in the latter, not only a body, but an immortal soul is denied existence in time and in eternity."

Margaret declared in her autobiography that the archbishop's address was "a monstrous doctrine . . . that children, misshapen, deformed, hideous to the eye, either mentally or constitutionally unequipped for life, should continue to

---

[210] Ibid., 297.

[211] Margaret Sanger, *The Pivot of Civilization* (New York: 1922), 1.

[212] Margaret Sanger, "The Sin of Birth Control," *The Birth Control Review*, February 1922, 17.

be born in the hope that Heaven might be filled!"[213] She mocked the address in an article titled "The Sin of Birth Control" published in her February 1922 issue of *The Birth Control Review.*[214]

Margaret disregarded the archbishop's words and expanded her Fifth Avenue office into a Clinical Research Bureau in 1925 and again in 1930, purchasing a three-story house in Manhattan. She continued bootlegging diaphragms from Europe until the German immigrant Julius Schmid began domestically manufacturing condoms, earning him the title of "the undisputed king of the American condom empire" in a 1938 publication of *Fortune* magazine.[215]

The bureau sent Dr. James F. Cooper on a lecture tour and secured the consent of twenty thousand US doctors willing to cooperative with their contraceptive advancements. Meanwhile, the bureau discovered that the ingredients in the German contraceptive jelly (chinosol and Irish moss) were too expensive. Dr. Cooper and Dr. Hannah M. Stone devised a cheaper formula, which Margaret recorded was "a jelly with a lactic acid and glycerine base."[216] Margaret declared, "I wanted . . . to push ahead until hospitals and public health agencies took over birth control as part of their regular program."[217]

---

[213]   Sanger, *The Autobiography of Margaret Sanger*, 309.

[214]   Margaret Sanger, "The Sin of Birth Control," *The Birth Control Review*, February 1922, 17.

[215]   Andrea Tone, *Devices and Desires: A History of Contraceptives in America* (New York: 2001), 187.

[216]   Sanger, *The Autobiography of Margaret Sanger*, 363.

[217]   Ibid.

Men Rule the East

Invited to Japan in 1921 as a main speaker in a lecture series with Albert Einstein, Bertrand Russell, and H. G. Wells, Margaret Sanger was not welcomed by the Japanese government. They feared that she was a US agent sent to deplete their population. This was further complicated by the Japanese translation of her last name, which was similar to *sangai san* or "destructive to production."[218] Agreeing not to publicly lecture on birth control, she was reluctantly admitted.

Margaret concluded that Japan was "undoubtedly a man's country." It was thick with ingrained prejudice and a domesticated outlook with no leanings toward rebellion. She recalled, "Only those who had turned Christian showed any signs of thinking independently." Japan's demand for cheap and unskilled labor proved that "practically half the female population, some thirteen millions, [from age ten] were engaged in gainful occupation though few were economically independent."[219]

Continuing to China, Margaret spoke at the Peking National University to "the most brilliant students of Young China." The university's chancellor led the anti-Christian movement, and her host, Dr. Hu-Shih, was the initiator of the Chinese Renaissance. She recorded a conversation with Hu-Shih and his friends in which the question was posed: "Why could [man] not produce a class of human beings unable to procreate? Was there any reason why the particular biological factors that made the mule sterile could not

---

218   Ibid., 324.
219   Ibid., 330.

be applied further? They discussed the interesting possibility of creating a neuter gender such as the workers in a beehive or ant hill."[220]

Sadly, Margaret found "the only method of family limitation known to the poor Chinese was infanticide of girl babies by suffocation or drowning. . . . When infanticide was stopped, the corresponding increase in sing-song girls making their living by prostitution was almost immediately evident."[221] One of the young prostitutes told her that she entertained as many as ten to twelve sailors a night when their ships docked. Margaret wrote, "I thought I would never recover from the shock of seeing American men spending their evenings at such places with what were obviously children."[222] Margaret concluded that China's incessant fertility was demonstrative of overpopulation, reducing the "once fountainhead of wisdom . . . to the dust by superabundant breeding."[223]

When she made her long-awaited trip to "famine-stricken" Russia in 1934, to see for herself "what was happening in the greatest social experiment of our age," she was disappointed.[224] Instead of finding a happy blend of economic Marxism and Malthusian philosophy, Margaret observed men doing the skilled work and women "kept at the laborious, monotonous, physical labor." Portraits of Lenin and Stalin adorned all public places, and the culture was so drenched in

---

[220]   Ibid., 342.
[221]   Ibid., 344–45.
[222]   Ibid., 346.
[223]   Ibid., 348.
[224]   Ibid., 433.

Marxian philosophy that it had traded its sense of beauty for one of purpose. Placing all hope in its youth, "Marxian ideology had been applied to every phase of life."[225] Visitors were led through a cathedral transformed into the Anti-Religious Museum with tours given by ten- to twelve-year-old girls elevating "the Soviet way."

In spite of this, Margaret curiously noted how "Russia was also aiming to free women from the two bonds that enslaved them most—the nursery and the kitchen."[226] Children were "priceless possessions" of the state and "no longer were they a drain or burden to their families."[227] Russia was "building a healthy race" and even food supply was given first to children, hospitals, Communists, and industrial professional classes, while "old people over fifty had to scrape along on what they could get."[228]

She discovered that the Russian Institute for Experimental Medicine was using spermatoxin to sterilize women for four to five months at a time. Yet, the Russian government still favored abortion. As Margaret noted, "Some of these women had had five abortions in two years and one had had eight."[229] Margaret concluded that if Russia's population problem was left unchecked, it "would multiply from the bottom unskilled, ignorant, dull-witted workers."[230] She left

---

225   Ibid., 440.
226   Ibid., 441–42.
227   Ibid., 442.
228   Ibid.
229   Ibid., 450.
230   Ibid., 451.

Russia questioning "whether exploitation by government or by individual was basically different."[231]

The Mother Within

Margaret's autobiography is hauntingly woven with the faint call of her absent family. Despite her clarity that her life's purpose was owed to the betterment of humanity through birth control, Margaret nevertheless struggled with her maternal desire. Throughout her work, she periodically longed for her children, who she willingly forsook for the cause. She confided in her autobiography, "Inevitably I have been constantly torn between my compulsion to do this work and a haunting feeling that I was robbing my children of time which they were entitled."[232]

Margaret's original desire for a large family and joyful home-life were often interrupted by her work. She recalled how her son Grant "whole-heartedly disapproved of [her] political activities" and often protested the Socialist meetings she left home to attend. As her birth control quest continued, Margaret spoke of how her children habitually searched for her after school, enthusiastically celebrating when they found her at home. But unable to supply them a consistent "measure of permanence," Margaret surrendered her active physical motherhood as an unfulfilled dream.[233]

She overlooked the frustrated remarks of allied reporters who said she should have "birth controlled" her own

---

231   Ibid., 459.
232   Ibid., 264.
233   Ibid., 94.

children. And those asking why she didn't "stay home and spend some thought on disciplining [her] own family."[234] Knowing her daughter's sad fate, I was pierced with compassion as Margaret struggled to desert her children and escape to England, writing that it was with "the faint hope that my efforts might, perhaps, make Peggy's future easier."[235] Her daughter Peggy, who Margaret said was "the embodiment of all my hopes in a daughter," lived her last two years on earth separated from her mother by an ocean's divide.

Margaret confessed being "tempted to slip back into peaceful domesticity" as her sons passed the years in the care of her family and servants. She wrote, "For several years I hung on to this dream of being with them constantly, but it was only a dream."[236] Believing that fate had other plans for her, Margaret chose to "sacrifice [her] maternal feelings" for her work. When their second house burned down, Margaret sent her young boys off to boarding schools, recalling that she "thereafter could only visit them over week-ends or on the rare occasions when I was speaking in the vicinity." She reflected, "At times the homesickness for them seemed too much to bear. . . . I wanted to be able to sink gratefully into the warmth and glow of a loving family welcome."[237]

Margaret took ten-year-old Grant with her to California over the winter of 1917–1918 as she wrote her book *Woman and the New Race*, which championed birth control

234   Ibid., 116.
235   Ibid., 122.
236   Ibid., 265.
237   Ibid., 265–66.

as "the revolt of women against sex servitude."[238] It's hard to imagine her reconnecting with her motherhood while simultaneously writing demands for voluntary motherhood, preaching the harmful effects of celibacy, and calling for a *birth ban* on parents with mentally or physically defective children. That summer, through her struggle to reconcile her motherhood with her contraceptive mission, Margaret concluded that "the most important force in the remaking of the world is a free motherhood."[239]

She then shocked America when she remarried the wealthy conservative churchman James Noah Slee in 1922, despite warning him that he "would always have to be kissing me good-by in depots or waving farewell as the gangplank went up."[240] But she confessed "a gathering loneliness in my life—not seeing the children except on holidays, never having time to spend with old friends or to make new ones." She and James built a lakeside home outside New York City with an exquisite garden, treetop studio, and horse stables. Margaret remarked of her posh new lifestyle that "domesticity, which I had once so scorned, had its charms after all."[241]

Her motherhood and work were again put at odds in 1929 when Margaret's son Stuart contracted a serious case of mastoiditis. Margaret left Stuart's bedside to investigate a police raid on her clinic. She sent Stuart to the hospital for an operation and reported having "even more misgivings" upon leaving him for her scheduled lecture tour. Stuart then

238 Margaret Sanger, *Woman and The New Race* (New York, 1920), 1.
239 Ibid., 7.
240 Sanger, *The Autobiography of Margaret Sanger*, 356.
241 Ibid., 357.

fractured the bone above his eye in 1933, which led to nine successive operations. Despite this, Margaret kept her plans to visit Russia but returned home when Stuart's illness grew worse. At the doctor's recommendation, Margaret took Stuart to Arizona in hopes that the dry climate would be healing. Margaret and Stuart lived together in Arizona for six months, causing her to reflect that "the joy of thus familiarizing myself with my grown-up son made me envy mothers who had leisure to grow along with their children or, at least, to watch them develop."[242]

Margaret dedicated *Woman and the New Race* to the memory of her own mother: "A mother who gave birth to eleven living children." Perhaps her mother's memory pressed her on. Margaret's father told her early in her contraceptive fight that "your mother would have been alive today if we had known all this then."[243] Somehow, through her unrelenting fight for voluntary motherhood, Margaret retained her convoluted belief that motherhood "is not only the oldest but the most important profession in the world."[244]

Eugenics

The eugenicist Haverlock Ellis wrote of birth control, "Like the wizard's lazy apprentice who foolishly released the stream he could not control, we have struggled vainly to stem the tide of unfit babies, and now at last we have learnt the magic formula to apply at the source."[245]

---

[242]   Ibid., 460.
[243]   Ibid., 115.
[244]   Sanger, *The Pivot of Civilization*, 28.
[245]   Havelock Ellis, "Birth Control and Eugenics," *The Eugenics Re-*

Was Margaret Sanger *truly* a eugenicist? She affirmed clearly that she was. Margaret's eugenic aim targeted the mentally and physically challenged as well as the poor. Her solution to ridding the population of such persons was found in the use of birth control and sterilization. Margaret stated in a 1919 article, "I personally believe in the sterilization of the feeble-minded, the insane and syphilitic."[246]

She possessed a deep eugenic prejudice toward the masses in ghettos and slums who "produce in their helplessness other helpless, diseased and incompetent masses."[247] Margaret unabashedly stated that "the fundamental convictions that form the basis of our Birth Control propaganda . . . indicate that the campaign for Birth Control is not merely of eugenic value, but is practically identical in ideal, with the final aims of Eugenics."[248] For Margaret, "Eugenics without Birth Control . . . is at the mercy of the rising stream of the unfit. . . . Only upon a free, self-determining motherhood can rest any unshakable structure of racial betterment."[249]

Margaret dedicated her first issue of *The Birth Control Review* on February 1917 "to the Principle of Intelligent and Voluntary Motherhood." She introduced the *Review*'s mission, stating, "No law is too sacred to break!" She included Moses, Christ, and Joan of Arc among humanity's past lawbreakers. [250] Margaret identified the modern plague as "a

---

view, April 1917, 37.

[246] Margaret Sanger, "Birth Control and Racial Betterment," *The Birth Control Review*, February 1919.

[247] Ibid.

[248] Margaret Sanger, "The Eugenic Value of Birth Control Propaganda," *The Birth Control Review*, October 1921, 5.

[249] Sanger, "Birth Control and Racial Betterment."

[250] Margaret Sanger, *The Birth Control Review*, vol. I, no. 1, February

disease sprung from ignorance of the means of preventing conception."[251] She challenged women to stop being the helpless victims of excessive childbearing and undesired motherhood.

The *Review's* next article, "Birth Control in Relation to Morality," was penned by British intellectual physician and eugenicist Havelock Ellis. Margaret dedicated a chapter of her autobiography to Havelock, comparing him to St. Francis of Assisi. She said, "To know him has been a bounteous privilege; to claim him friend my greatest honor."[252] Havelock likewise said Margaret was a "heroic pioneer" of humanity in elevating the race. She had discovered "the key to the eugenic position." Havelock said birth control was "the only instrument by means of which that eugenic selection can be rendered practicable."[253]

Margaret also spoke at the women's branch of the Ku Klux Klan in 1925. She often targeted inner-city minorities in her eugenics lectures, which Havelock claimed "so many of the chief branches of the white stock are being sapped in their racial vitality by influences of previously unknown virulence."[254] Havelock promoted vasectomy and tubal ligation for those deemed "unfit." He advised physicians to use seclusion on patients in order to "exert a gentle but firm pressure in emphasizing the advantages of the operation."[255] Claiming

---

          1917, 4.
[251]   Ibid.
[252]   Sanger, *The Autobiography of Margaret Sanger*, 141.
[253]   Ellis, "Birth Control and Eugenics," 34.
[254]   Ibid., 33.
[255]   Havelock Ellis, "The Sterilization of the Unfit," *The Eugenics Review*, 1909, 205.

that God did not command us to have children who were "fatally condemned to disease or premature death," Havelock wrote that the "social order . . . could not be reached or maintained except by the systematic control of offspring."[256]

Havelock called for "a widening of the grounds upon which abortion should be permitted" due to the likely hereditary disposition that children conceived in incest and rape would become violent criminals themselves.[257] He advised sterilization for those suffering a mental disorder, a grave physical disability, and those likely to transmit genetic mental disorders.[258] Havelock advised "zealously to spread the knowledge of contraceptive measures among those classes whose fatal fertility it is necessary to arrest."[259]

Margaret and Havelock both favored the eugenics of lazy, improvident, and diseased persons, agreeing that the two fundamental eugenic aims "are to impede the production of bad stocks and to favour the production of good stocks."[260] This could be accomplished by recording family heredity, popularizing methods of birth control, and applying a great degree of pressure on those who deliberately disagree. Havelock suggested, "This pressure may in the mildest degree consist of such elementary social inducements . . . proceeding

---

[256] Havelock Ellis, *The Birth Control Review*, vol. I, no. 1, February 1917, 6.

[257] Havelock Ellis, "Abortion and the Law," *The British Medical Journal*, July 23, 1938, 198.

[258] "Report of the Department Committee on Sterilization," *Mental Welfare*, vol. XV, no. 1, January 1934, 2.

[259] Havelock Ellis, "Birth Control and Eugenics," 34.

[260] Ibid., 36.

to sterilization when these inducements fail, and in the ultimate and extreme degree to complete segregation."[261]

Margaret Sanger believed that enlightened eugenicists such as Havelock should replace the high-minded theorists and clergy in disseminating information on parenthood to the masses. This, she believed, would "limit and discourage the over-fertility of the mentally and physically defective" and rectify "the unbalance between the birth rate of the 'unfit' [unhealthy, mentally-defective, and poor] and the 'fit' [healthy, educated, and wealthy]."[262]

Margaret wrote in a 1925 article, "We are spending billions, literally billions, keeping alive thousands who never, in all human compassion, should have been brought into this world. We are spending more in maintaining morons than in developing the inherent talents of gifted children. We are coddling the incurably defective and neglecting potential geniuses."[263] She said that this had resulted "because we have left the production of American children to chance, instead of bringing this most important of all human functions within the sphere of choice." She then quoted eugenic botanist Luther Burbank, who said, "America . . . is like a garden in which the gardener pays no attention to the weeds. Our criminals are our weeds, and weeds breed fast and are intensely hardy. They must be eliminated. Stop permitting criminals and weaklings to reproduce. . . . We nourish the unfit and criminal instead of exterminating them. Nature

---

261   Ibid., 41.
262   Sanger, "The Eugenic Value of Birth Control Propaganda," 5.
263   Margaret Sanger, "Is Race Suicide Probable?" *Colliers*, August 15, 1925.

eliminates the weeds, but we turn them into parasites and allow them to reproduce."[264]

Margaret's 1920 article "Women Enslaved by Maternity" warned that organized labor in America would never thrive "while those within it continue to bring hordes of human beings into the world."[265] It taught that women "enslaved by the function of maternity" cannot take an active role in social and political life, because "no woman who is bringing children into the world year after year can possibly take a real interest in matters outside the domestic circle."[266] True to her overpopulation beliefs, Margaret stated in her 1919 "Birth Control and Racial Betterment," "We who advocate Birth Control . . . lay all our emphasis upon stopping not only the reproduction of the unfit but upon stopping all reproduction when there is not economic means of providing proper care for those who are born in health."[267]

Margaret Sanger proclaimed, "We have got to strike at the roots of our social evils, and birth control is the only automatic cure for all social problems. . . . In a well-balanced society where we desire quality rather than quantity we shall not have the 'unwanted child.'"[268]

---

[264]   Sanger, "Is Race Suicide Probable?"

[265]   Margaret Sanger, "Women Enslaved by Maternity," *Lloyd's Sunday News*, May 16, 1920.

[266]   Sanger, "Women Enslaved by Maternity."

[267]   Sanger, "Birth Control and Racial Betterment."

[268]   Sanger, "Women Enslaved by Maternity."

Planned Parenthood

"I insisted that the first right of a child was to be wanted, to be desired, to be planned for with an intensity of love that gave it its title to being."[269]

—Margaret Sanger, Autobiography

Planned Parenthood claims today that "abortion is one of the safest medical procedures" and that "nearly one in three women will have an abortion" in their lifetime.[270] This is largely thanks to the efforts of Margaret Sanger, whose 1916 Colorado Birth Control chapter spawned Planned Parenthood. But how did Margaret Sanger, who repeatedly renounced abortion, become championed as the founder of the largest abortion provider in American history?

Margaret remained unfalteringly opposed to abortion throughout her life. She gave a speech in Charlottenburg-Berlin in 1927 declaring that "birth control has always been practiced, beginning with infanticide, which is abhorred, and then by abortion, nearly as bad."[271] On her 1934 Russian

---

[269] Sanger, *The Autobiography of Margaret Sanger*, 194.

[270] "100 Years," *Planned Parenthood*, https://100years.plannedparenthood.org/#e1956-1976/6, accessed March, 23, 2020.

[271] Sanger, *The Autobiography of Margaret Sanger*, 388.

visit, Margaret said, "In my opinion it is a cruel method of dealing with the problem because abortion, no matter how well done, is a terrific nervous strain and an exhausting physical hardship."[272] Margaret's vision for Planned Parenthood aligned with her desire to expand contraceptive clinics across America, not to provide abortions.

She was surprised to learn that German health insurance companies were underwriting sterilizations, recording, "I saw [Dr. Herthe Riese] order seventy-five of these major operations one evening between six o'clock and eight-thirty in her own clinic."[273] Margaret was exposed to abortion propaganda on a visit to Berlin in 1930, where she watched "a film which had traversed . . . Germany as propaganda for abortion under safe conditions."[274] She rented a theater in Geneva and showed the film at her 1930 conference to "physicians and directors of clinics from different parts of the world," demonstrating the tragic results in the absence of contraception.[275] Margaret considered the conference an international milestone in the birth control movement because "all propaganda, all moral and ethical aspects of the subject were forgotten . . . into the current of serene, impersonal, scientific abstraction."[276]

Margaret Sanger's Birth Control League and Research Bureau were dissolved into the Birth Control Federation of America, which in 1939 renamed itself Planned Parenthood.

---

[272]   Ibid., 449.
[273]   Ibid., 389.
[274]   Ibid., 409.
[275]   Ibid.
[276]   Ibid., 410.

Margaret proudly served as the first president of the International Planned Parenthood Federation from 1952 to 1959, as clinics began opening across the country. During her presidency, Margaret continually "condemned abortion as dangerous and inhuman," as stated in her 1956 article in *Reader's Digest*, "Asia Discovers Birth Control"[277]

Her era, which has been considered heroic by some, ended in sadness. Margaret lost the favor of her colleagues and suffered multiple heart attacks. She became dependent on the pain killer Demerol, sleeping pills, and alcohol. Margaret struggled with the attacks of friends and enemies alike, which caused her public disgrace as she slipped into dementia.[278] After a life dedicated to birth control, Margaret Sanger died of heart failure in 1966, just seven years before her efforts were overridden by the 1973 *Roe v. Wade* decision to legalize abortion. Planned Parenthood is now the largest provider of abortion, contraception, and sex education in the country. Margaret's "complicated" legacy is still honored yearly by Planned Parenthood through its Margaret Sanger Award, despite opposition from minority and religious groups.

Reproductive rights are now almost unequivocally linked to female empowerment and gender equality. History forgets the experimentation done in 1956 on Puerto Rican women, which resulted in harmful side effects. These women unknowingly underwent a large-scale human trial

---

[277]   Margaret Sanger, "Asia Discovers Birth Control," *Reader's Digest*, July 1956, 36-38.

[278]   Jonathan Eig, *The Birth of the Pill: How Four Crusaders Reinvented Sex and Launched a Revolution* (W.W. Noton & Company, 2014), 159.

of high-dose hormonal birth control and IUDs funded and directed by Planned Parenthood.[279] Birth control was also tested on institutionalized patients and inmates. Planned Parenthood claims, "At least 25% of women living on reservations are sterilized throughout the 1970's, many after being coerced, misinformed, or threatened."[280]

Planned Parenthood's eugenic genesis wove the American theory of reproductive freedom and voluntary motherhood with racial prejudice and involuntary sterilization. In 1936, Congress allowed the import, mailing, and use of contraceptives. This was followed in 1937 by the legal allowance of physicians to recommend contraceptives. By 1940, thirty American states had passed sterilization laws.[281] According to a 2014 piece in *Rutgers Race and Law Review,* "In the USA, more than half of the 50 states passed laws permitting the sterilization of people diagnosed with a mental illness and disabled persons, criminals, persons with specific physical illnesses, such as epilepsy, Native Americans, and African-Americans."[282] Author and researcher Jonathan Eig reported in his 2014 book *The Birth of the Pill: How Four Crusaders Reinvented Sex and Launched a Revolution* that the pill has lowered libidos, increased divorce rates, and increased global population by four billion.[283]

---

[279]   Angela Franks, *Margaret Sanger's Eugenic Legacy: The Control of Female Fertility* (McFarland & Company, Inc., 2005), 220.

[280]   "100 Years," *Planned Parenthood.*

[281]   Ian Robert Dowbiggin, *Keeping America Sane* (Cornell University, 1997), 6.

[282]   Tiesha Rashon Peal, "The Continuing Sterilization of Undesirables in America," *Rutgers Race and Law Review,* 2004.

[283]   Eig, *The Birth of the Pill,* 164.

Where was the Catholic Church? The 2013 book *Sterilized by the State* claimed that "frustrated contributors to eugenic journals lamented that 'the Roman Catholic Church "furnished the main opposition" to bills in New York and Connecticut, and eugenic laws in general.'"[284] It further reported that "the 'relentless opposition' of The Roman Catholic Church eventually 'sapped the enthusiasm for state laws.'"[285] The Catholic Church opposed Margaret Sanger's belief that a person's "title to being" is measured by the desire and planning of one's parents. The Church also opposed voluntary and involuntary sterilizations and eugenic aims. Catholic doctrine upholds the teaching that the intentional destruction of innocent life is evil in all circumstances. The suffragettes agreed with the Catholic Church on abortion. Many women continue to discover the value of human life at all stages in order to preserve the true freedom and equal rights of women and of all humanity.

---

284   Randall Hansen and Desmond King, *Sterilized by the State: Eugenics, Race, and the Population Scare in Twentieth-Century North America* (New York: Cambridge University Press, 2013), 132.

285   Ibid., 135.

The Sexual Revolution

*"A Liberated Woman was somebody who had sex before marriage
and a job afterward. . . . Liberation isn't exposure to the American
values of Mom-and-apple-pie anymore; it's the escape from them."*[286]

—Gloria Steinem, 1969

The Sexual Revolution was an absurdly dead experiment of the past by the time I was in high school. There was nothing appealing about free-love orgies or being used for my body by some pot-smoking loser in the back of a Winnebago as part of his sexual expedition. The whole generation was summed up as "hippies" and dismissed with a superior air of confidence. Feminism seemed to have *matured* since then. We still didn't want to *be* men, but we wanted the generative freedom men had, and contraception had artificially granted us that. Sex had absolutely no conditions or consequences, and more importantly, it was no longer in the hands of men. Women were free from their slavish child-bearing duties to go out into the world and pursue meaningful work that paid others to educate their children. My high school teachers were quick to adopt this progressive way of

---

[286]   Gloria Steinem, "After Black Power, Women's Liberation," *New York Magazine*, April 4, 1969.

thinking, although their classrooms still held remnants of the sexual revolution and its philosophies were slipped into every subject.

Meanwhile, I was actively writing songs on my guitar and constructing lyrics that were strongly influenced by the riot grrrl movement. I struck up a friendship with an unlikely feminist who was tall and beautiful as well as seemingly stable and close with her parents. She played bass and was also deeply into the riot grrrl movement, so we formed a band. Not long after that, I was sought out by a chain-smoking, rough-around-the-edges rocker girl rumored to be a lesbian. She also happened to be an amazing drummer. She became the third member of our band as well as my closest friend.

Our female punk conglomerate was formed, and we began practicing daily in our bass player's basement. We booked shows at VFWs and at local underground anarchist punk festivals where we were often the only girl band. As we gained momentum, our band branched out to playing clubs and collaborating with other riot grrrl bands. After years of playing and networking, we launched our first CD and loaded our gear into a van that would tour the United States.

There came a point in time when I realized that the Sexual Revolution was not as dead as I had believed it to be. More likely, the Sexual Revolution's free-love philosophy was proof of contraception's influence on our culture. We had deconstructed the '50s housewife into a derogatory symbol of servitude. She was cartoonishly caricatured as a domestic slave in high heels and pearls, yet eternally draped in an apron. Pornography was "main-stream," and pornographic elements in art and music demonstrated a full use of our artistic license. Being scandalized was evidence of artistic immaturity, which inhibited creativity. Our revolt against society's exploitation of women had ironically led us to take the upper hand in exploiting ourselves.

Saving sex for marriage was an archaic form of sexism perpetuated by Christianity. The sooner you overcame the obstacle of proving the insignificance of sex in your life, the better. As author Dawn Eden Goldstein reflected in her 2019 autobiographical work *Sunday Will Never Be the Same*, "My virginity had become an albatross, an embarrassing keepsake of my juvenile dreams. It made me self-conscious and kept me from being able to interact with a potential boyfriend like a normal person."[287] The effects of the Sexual Revolution on feminism were everlasting. Virginity became a barrier to claiming feminism.

Simone de Beauvoir

"One is not born, but rather becomes, woman. No biological, psychic, or economic destiny defines the figure that the human female takes on in a society; it is civilization as a whole that elaborates this intermediary product between the male and the eunuch that is called feminine."[288]

Feminism in America continued to affiliate with violent tendencies and pro-choice ideologies. Its theorists promoted existentialism, which taught that human beings created their own identity and value rather than inherently possessing

---

[287]   Dawn Eden Goldstein, *Sunday Will Never be the Same* (Catholic Answers, 2019), 115.
[288]   Simone de Beauvoir, *The Second Sex* (Vintage Books, 2011), 283.

them. Simone de Beauvoir was *the* atomic bomb of feminism. If Madame Restell's historic ethical defiance paved the way for dehumanizing the person and rejecting faith, then Simone de Beauvoir gave it enduring permanence. The famous French philosopher had a stirring influence on the formation of feminist theory.

Simone was born into a wealthy Catholic family in 1908 and attended an elite convent school. She considered a religious vocation before completely losing her faith as a teen and rejecting all religions as inventions that projected male dominance. Simone de Beauvoir was later said by American biographer Judith Thurman to be "as devout an atheist as she had once been a Catholic."[289]

A gifted intellectual, Simone studied philosophy at Sorbonne University in Paris. She met the existentialist Jean-Paul Sartre, and thereafter the two remained in an open bisexual relationship, which sometimes included their students. Simone's 1943 novel *She Came to Stay* was based on one of the couple's ménage à trois.[290]

Simone believed that marriage and motherhood threatened women's integrity. She shared this thesis in her ground-breaking eight-hundred-page encyclopedia, which has often been referred to as the "feminist bible." *Le Deuxième Sexe* (*The Second Sex*) was published in French in 1949 and in English in 1953. As the Sexual Revolution ripened in America, it became infused with Simone's existentialist beliefs. *The Second Sex* uncovered the dark roots

---

[289]   Ibid., xii.
[290]   Ibid., xi.

of an oppressive male society, debunked religious myths and decried the long-enduring female slavery perpetuated through patriarchy. Simone destroyed the concept of both "woman" and "femininity," fusing her theories of women's struggle with their scornful physical identity and reproductive curse. *The Second Sex* produced an avalanche of future crises for women.

Simone began her exploration of femininity in *The Second Sex* with the same opening question posed by this book: "What is a woman?"[291] While recognizing the obvious physical distinctions of the female to the male sex, Simone concluded that there *is* not and never *was* such a thing as femininity. Instead, the characteristics ascribed to femininity are secondary reactions projected on girls and are therefore "situational." According to Simone, femininity is not innate in any way. She believed that women were originally defined as an inessential "Other: [and] an attempt is made to freeze her as an object."[292] In striking resemblance to modern gender theory, Simone said, "The female is a woman, insofar as she feels herself as such."[293] Therefore, *exalting* a woman "in the name of femininity, [is] the surest way to disserve her."[294]

The Second Sex explored the subordination of women by men throughout history, literature, religion, education, economy, and culture. Simone sought to prove the perpetual separation of men and women into "two castes."[295] The male

291 Ibid., 3.
292 Ibid., 17.
293 Ibid., 49.
294 Ibid., 130.
295 Ibid., 154.

caste enjoyed favor and the transmission of paternal rights and property within the patriarchal family. Women were forced into domestic slavery. Simone taught that a woman wins her dignity as a human being when she "escapes the home and plays a new role in industrial production." Still, she struggled with the problem of women "reconciling the reproductive role and productive work. . . . The fundamental reason . . . is her enslavement to the generative function."[296]

Simone faulted Christianity for society's moral abortion conflict. She said, "It was Christianity that overturned moral ideas on this point by endowing the embryo with a soul; so abortion became a crime against the fetus itself."[297] She dispelled the guilt of abortion and rejected the Catholic position against abortion and contraception. Simone believed that "with artificial insemination, the evolution that will permit humanity to master the reproductive function comes to completion."[298] Simone de Beauvoir's philosophy embraced reproductive control through abortion, contraception, and artificial insemination. Through these, "woman in her turn is freed from nature; she wins control of her body. . . . The convergence of these two factors—participation in production and freedom from reproductive slavery—explains the evolution of women's condition."[299] She predicted the results of this reproductive evolution in America, stating

---

[296]   Ibid., 136.
[297]   Ibid., 137.
[298]   Ibid., 139.
[299]   Ibid., 139.

that "divorce is going to flourish, and husbands and wives are no more than provisional associates."[300]

Simone vehemently denounced the "essence" of femininity, which she believed to falsely ascribe passivity, flirtatiousness, and an innate desire for motherhood to the female. She rejected fostering these qualities in girls, as well as forbidding affections to boys (sometimes leading to homosexuality) and emboldened them with superiority through the privilege of having a penis.[301] She believed that as girls discovered the social meaning of the words "pretty" and "ugly," they were taught to objectify themselves to please others. Simone even asserted that these traits were imposed on daughters by mothers "bent on transforming her into women like themselves with zeal and arrogance mixed with resentment."[302] According to Simone, the female "is a human being before becoming a woman."[303] She is imposed with a prototypical "feminine" destiny, which reveals that "because she is woman, the girl knows that the sea and the poles, a thousand adventures, a thousand joys, are forbidden to her; she is born on the wrong side."[304]

The magic of motherhood then fades during puberty, as *The Second Sex* revealed: "Often it seems not extraordinary at all but rather horrible that a parasitic body should proliferate inside her body."[305] The teenage girl is embarrassed

[300]   Ibid., 140.
[301]   Ibid., 287.
[302]   Ibid., 295.
[303]   Ibid., 308.
[304]   Ibid., 311.
[305]   Ibid., 312.

to discover that sex is a dirty and shameful act. She suc-
cumbs to the abnormal pain and horror of menstruation
with humiliation and "disgust for her body." Simone said
that the female "puberty crisis" reveals to her that "the only
novelty is the disgusting event repeated monthly."[306] Further,
"the menstrual stain inclines her toward disgust and fear."
Females discover this to be *their* right of passage and the
definition of "being a woman!"[307]

The Second Sex painted the picture of a girl's innocent
fantasy of love being awakened to the reality of the male's
"biologically aggressive role" in sex. Simone wrote, "The
marriage structure, like the existence of prostitutes, proves
it: the woman *gives herself*; the man remunerates her and
takes her."[308] Sex is the "surgical" experience inevitably proving that "however deferential and courteous a man might
be, the first penetration is always a rape."[309] But according to
Simone, the element that "changes the sexual act into a grave
danger: [is] the danger of a child."[310] In this case, "the male
sperm becomes a harmful germ, a soiling." Only the use of
contraception and abortion can "make for far greater abandon during the love act."[311] She also observed that because
female pleasure was not usually a factor in heterosexual love
making, "nearly all girls have lesbian tendencies."[312]

---

[306]   Ibid., 326.
[307]   Ibid., 329.
[308]   Ibid., 386.
[309]   Ibid., 395.
[310]   Ibid., 398.
[311]   Ibid., 399.
[312]   Ibid., 355.

Rejecting God, Simone found men and women to be finite and arbitrary. Their "femininity" and "masculinity" were assigned social constructs based on physical strength, biology, and the need for one to oppress the other. But "Christian ideology played no little role in women's oppression," according to Simone. She said that Christianity relatively respected women in secondary and subordinate roles, but they still remained incomplete beings, without autonomy, created for men; "her spouse is her origin and finality."[313]

The Catholic Church was "the most troubling of influences" for Simone. She said, "The pope, the bishop whose ring is kissed, the priest who says Mass, the preacher, the person one kneels before in the secrecy of the confessional—these are men."[314] She believed the reason women threw themselves willingly into religion was because it filled a profound and unmet need for equality. Yet, it was women's passivity and renunciation that was sanctified through religion, allowing her participation in "a masochism that promises her supreme conquests." Simone rejected the teaching that love is women's assigned vocation. She believed that the nun chose God as her spiritual spouse in aiming to redeem her femininity through humiliation and suffering. The nun believes that God has "chosen" her, and "she feels filled with a mission." Yet, even the spiritual spouse fails to escape her subjectivity, and rather, "in the humiliation of God, she admires Man's fall."[315]

---

[313]   Ibid., 161.
[314]   Ibid., 304.
[315]   Ibid., 715.

Simone was both troubled and fascinated by the Catholic teaching that "virginity is the highest form of the feminine mystery." She concluded that all men naturally dissociate their wives from being mothers. Christians further this divide by turning "the body into the soul's enemy" and incarnating all temptations in women. Simone rejected the Christian teaching that man could not sexually approach a woman without purification rites and sacramental ceremonies. She also supposed that the Mother of Christ was a virgin in order to save her Son from the "stain of birth" rather than she, herself, being saved and fulfilling a prophetic miracle. She said, "The supreme masculine victory is consummated in the cult of Mary," whose character as a wife is rejected by removing her carnal nature and making her a docile servant.[316]

Queens by divine right and saints by their shining virtues were the only exceptions of women historically allowed to be men's equal, according to Simone. St. Catherine of Siena and St. Teresa of Avila were two examples she used in demonstrating the lives of women who lived their astonishing destiny independent of men. Still, Simone lamented, "so many men for one Joan of Arc; and behind her stands the great male figure of Saint Michael the archangel."[317]

"Marriage kills love," wrote Simone de Beauvoir, and women become even more subjective *in* marriage.[318] Men turn their desirous sex object into a captive wife, whereby she's no longer desirable to her husband and "weighed down by childbirth, she loses her sexual attraction." Spouses reach

---

[316]   Ibid., 189.
[317]   Ibid., 303.
[318]   Ibid., 204.

the point of engaging in "a kind of mutual masturbation," as "fidelity has meaning only as long as it is spontaneous."[319] In the absence of eroticism, she concluded, the wife becomes "less a lover than as the mother of their children." Simone championed feminists for transitioning modern women out of the home, where she believed women sacrifice themselves to a passionless and repetitive mediocrity. These women make their husbands the victims of their guilt. They desperately try to express themselves through home décor in a stifled attempt to "convert her prison into a heaven of glory." Her home becomes *her,* and "because she *does* nothing, she avidly seeks herself in what she *has*."[320]

Simone's feminism found hope in a motherhood less dependent on biological chance and more by design. She demanded that abortion "has to be considered one of the risks normally involved in the feminine condition." Simone was disgusted by antifeminists who refused to "accept that the fetus belonged to the mother carrying it." She rejected the claim that the fetus had a soul, stating, "[The pregnant woman] experiences [pregnancy] both as an enrichment and a mutilation; the fetus is part of her body, and it is a parasite exploiting her."[321] Maternal love is not natural, according to Simone, but perceived through artificial morality. "Breeders," as she called them, who willingly repeat childbearing indefinitely, seek to justify their existence through their passive fertility. Although she found Communist and Socialist countries to lighten the "burdens of motherhood"

---

[319]   Ibid., 467.
[320]   Ibid., 471.
[321]   Ibid., 538.

by recognizing maternity as a social function and entrusting the care and education of children to the state, women continued to remain both worker and housekeeper.

Simone de Beauvoir, like Margaret Sanger and Madame Restell before her, was influenced by the famous utilitarian John Stuart Mill. Like Sanger, she also regarded the eugenicist Havelock Ellis. Utilitarian and eugenic principles greatly influenced the formation of these leading feminist philosophies, many of which are still retained in feminism today. Simone's philosophy on women has shaped feminist theory and encouraged women to create or reject their femininity at will. Simone's principles to "remake woman" require the rejection of femininity and masculinity and have influenced the gender-neutral approach to raising children. Her ideal of equality for women spans education, work, and erotic freedom. It demands equal access to birth control and abortion and defines marriage as a free engagement to be broken at any time. Simone believed that women should not be in the home and that society must be responsible for its children.

In a shocking 1975 interview with Betty Friedan, Simone de Beauvoir stated, "No woman should be authorized to stay at home to raise her children. . . . Women should not have that choice, precisely because if there is such a choice, too many women will make that one." She went on to say, "It is a way of forcing women in a certain direction."[322] Betty Friedan disagreed with Simone's rigidity (and bigotry) in not allowing women the *choice* to stay home. Simone insisted

---

[322]   Betty Friedan, *It Changed My Life: Writings on the Women's Movement* (Cambridge: Harvard University Press, 1998), 397.

that this was the only way to free women and change society. She said, "As long as the family and the myth of family and the myth of maternity and the maternal instinct are not destroyed, women will still be oppressed."[323]

The Feminine Mystique

I still remember how *angry* I was at the end of the movie *A League of Their Own* when Dottie, a.k.a. "The Queen of Diamonds," decided not to play in the first Women's World Series because her husband returned home from war. I passionately shared the sentiments of her coach, played by Tom Hanks, appalled that she could walk away from the game to go and start a family. I saw Dottie's husband, Bob, as an impediment to the fulfillment of her dreams and talents. He was the *bad guy* swooping in to steal her from her victory and enslave what I saw as an outrageous combination of talent and whit to a brood of needy children in some remote Oregon town. I felt heartbroken at the monotonous life that awaited her and the definitive sadness she would inevitably discover. There was a helplessness in watching the star character slip away to the drudgery of family life after proving herself worthy of so much more. I felt as though I were living her future regret for her and vowed never to make it my own.

In 1963, American feminist Betty Friedan published *The Feminine Mystique*. Momentum from her revolutionary work propelled her to found the National Organization for Women (NOW) three years later in 1966. *The Feminine*

---

[323]   Ibid.

Mystique questioned the stifling role of American housewives and had an electrifying effect on the second wave of
feminism. Betty prefaced her book with a simple question
that she believed was on the lips of many American women:
"Is this all?"

Betty surveyed countless women who seemed to be universally deceived from their earliest girlhood into believing
they could attain "true feminine fulfillment" through "finding a husband and bearing children." Betty lamented, "They
learned that truly feminine women do not want careers,
higher education, political rights—the independence and
the opportunities that the old-fashioned feminists fought
for."[324] As a result, Betty noted that by the mid '50s, 60 percent of women had dropped out of college to marry and
many had confessed to attending college in hopes of finding a husband in the first place. The suburban wife had
become the "dream image" of young American girls who
were struggling to shrink their body size, dyeing their hair
blonde, and refusing to enter scientific fields because they
were "unfeminine."

Men found the inferiority problem of American women
to be settled, according to Betty, by their simple proclamation that women were "different but equal" from men.
Women struggled to believe this as they were offered limited
and conditional job opportunities and half of a man's salary.
Betty discovered a deeper, growing problem among American women, which she termed in her book "the problem

---

[324]   Betty Friedan, *The Feminine Mystique* (W.W. Norton & Company, 1997), 9.

that has no name." This problem consisted of an emptiness and an incompleteness, which led women to the feeling that she didn't really exist.

The problem that has no name became so common that it was referred to as "the housewife's syndrome." Housewives admitted to a dissatisfied feeling of entrapment that was at odds with the glorified versions of housewives being portrayed across 1960s television. Betty remarked that overeducated housewives were sympathetically judged to understand the value of everything except their own worth. Unhappy housewives were scorned for their unhappiness, which was said to be inevitably the result of "women's rights."

Betty recalled in *The Feminine Mystique* that "no other road to fulfillment was offered to American women in the middle of the twentieth century. . . . Most adjusted to their role and suffered or ignored the problem that has no name."[325] Refusing to accept this problem as a natural part of women's condition, Betty rejected the absurd theories that women would lose their femininity by participation in work outside of the home. Her book also revealed that the problem would not be solved by a bigger house or another baby. As a mother of three, Betty commiserated with the housewife who was simultaneously a business manager, cook, nurse, chauffeur, dressmaker, interior decorator, accountant, caterer, teacher, private secretary, and philanthropist, yet found no sense of purpose in it.[326] Betty's book unveiled the revelation that many American mothers were dissatisfied with their lives,

---

[325]   Ibid., 15.
[326]   Ibid., 90.

and although they loved their families, were regretful of giving up on past dreams.

The Feminine Mystique revolted against the traditional gender roles of the American family and the belief that fatigue and boredom were simply the "lot" of the housewife-mother. Betty sympathized with the chronically tired mothers who were working sixteen hours a day for seven days a week. She accused the husbands who hesitated to help around the house with "women's work" while their wives survived on prescribed tranquilizers and diet pills. Betty's book struck a deep chord that resonated with 1960s housewives who were secretly fearful of losing their identity in the daily and thoughtless grind of household drudgery.

As angry as I was with the original choice made by the character Dottie in the movie *A League of Their Own*, I came to discover through personal experience that choosing love can bear greater freedom than personal gain. But 1960s feminists were justifiably angry with the perceived lack of personal freedom and the media images constantly telling the housewife and mother "who she is, or can be, or wants to be."[327] Betty was the countercultural voice proclaiming that women were "unique human beings, not men with something missing."[328]

Betty realized that women's feminine capabilities went far beyond childbirth and encouraged women to forget about conforming to "the beautiful feminine picture" and to discover *themselves*. *The Feminine Mystique* allowed women to

---

[327]   Ibid., 126.
[328]   Ibid., 221.

worry less about perfection and more about *enjoying* their children and husbands as well as their creative work. Betty told women to stop joining unsatisfying committees or redecorating for the hundredth time. She also told women to fight against being treated as second-class citizens in professional fields and against sex discrimination in society.[329] Betty advised each woman to find her own answer to the problem without a name and to become fulfilled as human beings who were separate from their spouses and children.

The "housewife's feminism" perpetuated by *The Feminine Mystique* slowly caught on as media heroines began entering the workforce in fashionable business suits. The suburban wife was no longer the "dream image" of young American girls, who were already subscribing to the cultural belief that housewives were unhappily longing for a life outside of the home. Mothers began to encourage their daughters to pursue personal independence and focus on their education and career before starting a family. According to Betty, when women discovered that they had fallen victim to the *feminine mystique* of being their husband's wives and their children's mothers as the totality of who they were, they would either wither or awaken their creative ambition and begin contributing to the world.

The Feminine Mystique began its last chapter with the revelation that "there is no answer to the question 'who am I' except the voice inside herself."[330] Betty Friedan encouraged women to escape the "comfortable concentration camps" of

329   Ibid., 243.
330   Ibid., 220.

"the housewife trap and truly find fulfillment as wives and mothers."[331] She cautioned that women entering the workforce would face resistance from religious orthodoxy as well as husbands and friends. Betty consoled women, saying, "Once she begins to see through the delusions of the feminine mystique—and realizes that neither her husband nor her children, nor the things in her house, nor sex, nor being like all the other women, can give her a self—she often finds the solution much easier than she anticipated."[332] Women could create a new life plan that involved marriage, motherhood, and a "lifelong personal purpose," Betty argued.

The Feminine Mystique sought to "open the eyes" of American women. It professed that marriage and motherhood *would* disappoint women who expected their husbands and children to fulfill their lives entirely. Husbands and children could not fulfill all of women's voids, and according to Betty, this mentality caused irritation and discontent. Women felt "alive" through creative work and the discovery of their unique purpose in society, according to *The Feminine Mystique*. In many ways, Betty Friedan became the feminist champion of married American women and mothers. She reached into their perfectly manicured houses and identified their growing boredom as *the problem that has no name*. Her approach was neither as radical nor as shrouded in ultimatum as those of Sanger and Beauvoir, making her palpable to the average housewife. And while Betty advocated for birth control and abortion, she also respected the choices

---

[331]   Ibid., 219.
[332]   Ibid., 220.

of women to become wives and mothers while simultaneously encouraging them to pursue interests outside of the
home. Many radical feminists however, disassociated with
Betty Friedan for referring to lesbians in the women's rights
movement as "the lavender menace" and excluding lesbian
groups from NOW's Congress to Unite Women.[333]

Cosmo

Helen Gurley Brown hit society from a different feminist
angle. Helen took over as editor-in-chief of *Cosmopolitan*
magazine in 1965 and completely transformed the magazine's image. She rewrote Betty Friedan's housewife narra-
tive by promoting the racy, modern, single-career woman.
Proudly feminist, Helen spent thirty-two years forming the
new *Cosmo*, taking feminism one step further and focusing
on erasing the stigma of guilty sex outside of marriage.

Cosmo's more than blush-worthy pages included drawings
of sexual positions, articles promoting risky and scandalous
sex encounters, and displayed the best sex toys on the market. Burt Reynolds made his unforgettable debut in *Cosmo's*
1972 issue as its nude centerfold. Naturally, Helen's articles
boasted the benefits of birth-control for women's endless
sexcapades. She advised young women in her 1962 book *Sex
and the Single Girl, The Unmarried Woman's Guide to Men*,
"I think marriage is insurance for the worst years of your

---

[333]   Susan Brownmiller, "Sisterhood Is Powerful," *The New York Times*,
         March 15, 1970.

life. . . . [Men] are often cheaper emotionally and a lot more fun by the dozen."[334]

Helen's book became a wildly successful literary hit, which later inspired the characters for Candace Bushnell's 1997 *Sex and the City*. In her opening chapter, Helen flaunted the movie producer she had nabbed, the two Mercedes-Benzes, acres of San Francisco forest, Mediterranean house, and full-time maid she had acquired—all by the ripe old age of thirty-seven, after a successful and fulfilling single life.[335]

Single American women deceptively discovered in *Sex and the Single Girl* what married women had found in *The Feminine Mystique*: compassion for their state in life. Helen publicly voiced how the single girl's whole existence seemed to be "an apology for *not* being married."[336] Instead, Helen painted her as a glamour girl with a career and endless freedom. Helen's image of the single girl rejoiced in not being tied down to a husband and kids too soon. Her prototypical "single girl" was attractive precisely because she was not a wife or mother, allowing her "a better sex life than most of her married friends."[337] *Sex and the Single Girl* reveled in teasing men to the point of being "maddeningly hypocritical and, after arousing desire, insist that it be shut off by stating she wants to be chaste for the man she marries."[338] But Helen scolded the reality of chaste ambitions as well as

---

[334]   Helen Gurley Brown, *Sex and the Single Girl, The Unmarried Woman's Guide to Men* (Open Road Media, 2012), 19.
[335]   Ibid., 15.
[336]   Ibid., 16.
[337]   Ibid., 18.
[338]   Ibid., 22.

women who accidentally married homosexuals, which she said "comes from not having slept with the man you're going to marry, which is complete lunacy."[339]

Cosmo wasn't only selling sex, it was selling "sexy." Helen preached that being overweight or unattractive went hand-in-hand with being unhappily single and sexless. The *Cosmo* girl accordingly made dieting a fine art. Helen preached that the single girl was not to be pitied but rather highly respected and even envied. She told young women to work "like a son of a bitch" in developing their image. This included a fashionable style, having some brains and a private apartment, cooking well and having an interesting job, but most importantly, "your figure can't harbor an ounce of baby fat."[340] Helen also advised "not to rule out married men but to keep them as pets. . . . You 'use' *them* to add spice to your life."[341]

Helen Gurley Brown's feminism was oddly in favor of women objectifying themselves as well as the men in their lives. The *Cosmo* girl was a new and confident feminist who wasn't afraid of remaining single *and* enjoying sex. This base feminism promoted by Helen's *Cosmo* believed that the key to happiness was found in making the most out of life, as *Sex and the Single Girl* said, "whether it's two in the balcony or one on the aisle."[342]

---

[339]   Ibid., 40.
[340]   Ibid., 22.
[341]   Ibid., 36.
[342]   Ibid., 327.

Ms.

In stark contrast to *Cosmo*'s playgirl feminist, *Ms.* magazine once again rewrote the social rules for American women and successfully translated "a movement into a magazine."[343] The front cover of the preview issue of *Ms.* magazine in 1972, co-founded by Gloria Steinem, showed a weeping pregnant mother-goddess with eight arms doing household chores while wearing red heels. The title articles boasted "The Housewife's Moment of Truth," "Sisterhood," "On Raising Kids Without Sex Roles," "Sylvia Plath's Last Major Works," and "Women Tell the Truth About Their Abortions." The Comstock Laws could no longer silence them as they had silenced brazen activists in the past. As feminist journalist Susan Brownmiller wrote in her 1970 *New York Times* article, "The new feminism has taken hold . . . among urban, white, college educated, middle-class women generally considered to be a rather 'privileged' lot by those who thought they knew their politics, or knew their women."[344]

Ms. magazine realized that the 1970s women's liberation movement needed the revolt of American housewives in order to be successful. Its preview issue targeted and challenged housewives to "*Think revolutionary thoughts.*"[345] It urged them to insist that their husbands share the housework and childcare. The issue advised women to consider

---

[343]   "About Ms.," *Ms.*, https://msmagazine.com/about/, accessed May, 3, 2020.

[344]   Susan Brownmiller, "Sisterhood Is Powerful," *The New York Times*, March 15, 1970.

[345]   Jane O'Reilly, "The Housewife's Moment of Truth," *Ms.*, Spring/1972.

conveniences such as dishwashers and washing machines in order to free their time and discover their own ambitions. The magazine's strong message called housewives to become "liberated women" who "are not defined by our children and our husbands, but by ourselves."[346]

"We have had abortions" was the title of another article. It bemoaned the absurdity that women were still fighting for the "simple procedure" of abortion and the legal recognition "that a woman has the right to sovereignty over her own body."[347] The article included a petition to eliminate "the stigma still wrongly attached to abortion" and stated that approximately "one million American women have had 'illegal' abortions in 1971—many of them self-induced or performed by the unqualified, some of them fatal."[348] Gloria Steinem's name along with the names of Billie Jean King and the article's author were listed under the petition's fifty-three women who had had abortions.

Ms. also included a lesbian article in its preview issue. The article, "Can Women Love Women?" challenged socially imposed sex roles, "not only by discarding old notions of what should be considered 'natural,' but by offering a definition of relationships based only on human qualities and capabilities."[349] *Ms.* magazine supported the belief that women should be free to love another person (man or woman) as she chooses.

---

346   Ibid.
347   Barbaralee D. Diamonstein, "We have had abortions," *Ms.*, Spring/1972.
348   Ibid.
349   Anne Koedt, "Can Women Love Women?" *Ms.*, Spring/1972.

Despite *Ms.* initially seeming too radical for the average American woman, the magazine took root and successfully mainstreamed a "popular feminism" in the 1970s and '80s. *Ms.* magazine wove together strands of cultural and liberal feminism "with the need to eradicate sex roles, sex stereotyping, and legal inequalities in order to break down barriers to full participation in the mainstream," according to the book *Yours in Sisterhood: Ms. Magazine and the Promise of Popular Feminism.*[350] Feminism had not only become mainstream, but it was popular. The impact of its founder, Gloria Steinem—who discussed marriage as a form of part-time prostitution and said, "If men could get pregnant, abortion would be a sacrament"[351]—was extraordinary on the American feminist movement. Gloria put a target on the white, heterosexual, middle-class American male and encouraged women to embrace total independence, reject tradition and patriarchy, and instead *become* the men they wanted to marry.[352]

---

[350]   Amy Erdman Farrell, *Yours in Sisterhood: Ms. Magazine and the Promise of Popular Feminism* (University of North Carolina Press, 1998).

[351]   Emma Brockes, *"Gloria Steinem: 'If men could get pregnant, abortion would be a sacrament',"* *The Guardian*, October 17, 2015.

[352]   Gloria Steinem, *"Leaps of Consciousness,"* September, 2004.

The Catholic Response

"If, of the things taught by the Church, he holds what he chooses to hold, and rejects what he chooses to reject, he no longer adheres to the teaching of the Church as to an infallible rule, but to his own will."[353]

—St. Thomas Aquinas

I was thirty years old when I met my husband, and marriage followed pretty quickly. Although we diligently recorded every word that was said in our Natural Family Planning classes, we also knew that we wanted children, and lots of them, so we were elated to be pregnant six months into marriage. That first labor, however, was nothing like I had hoped or imagined. I faced many traumatic complications leading up to his birth, which was met with an ultimate thanksgiving for our son's life. Recovery was a slow and painful process in the fearful wake of ever considering birth again.

It was winter and our family was new to the area. We hadn't made many friends, and the months of being cooped up indoors with a fussy baby were mentally exhausting. When our son was only six months old, despite nursing-on-demand and tracking my fertility, we found out that we

---

[353] Thomas Aquinas, *Summa Theologiae*, II, q. 5, a. 3.

were expecting again. I panicked and immediately became anxious about the possibility of facing another traumatic labor. I toted around a baby for the next nine months as my belly and my mounting fear grew bigger. Our second son was born the night before a blizzard, and his birth was much easier than my first.

But the daunting reality of having two children under the age of two in our small townhouse began to sink in as my husband returned to work. I found myself gazing out the window at the cold mounting snow and bursting unexpectedly into hysterics. When women from church stopped by to drop off a meal, I would practically corner them, insisting they stay and talk. It was overwhelming as I began struggling with a feeling of immense guilt. I was terrified of being alone for even a moment because I couldn't control my racing thoughts and feared I was losing my mind.

Thankfully, my husband recognized my condition as postpartum depression. Also, our culture has moved past sterilizing, lobotomizing, and institutionalizing women such as me. My condition turned out to be physical and not mental. I was experiencing a stark depletion of progesterone (which had enhanced the function of serotonin receptors in my brain during pregnancy). My OB prescribed a bio-identical progesterone with an almost immediate onset, which 95 percent of patients, including me, responded to positively![354]

The next morning, I felt *completely* back to normal and continued taking the progesterone for another month. Still,

---

[354]   Thomas W. Hilgers, *The NaProtechnology Revolution* (New York: Beaufort Books, 2010).

my husband and I needed to figure out how to better space our children before no amount of progesterone would help me. We tried abstaining and learning a new method of Natural Family Planning, but to our shock and amazement, when our second son was just seven months old, we found out that we were pregnant a third time!

My emotions threatened to march over me like an enemy army for the next few months. I grappled with the situation of having three babies under three. Well-meaning friends came out of the woodwork with the compassionate suggestion that "although we had tried to follow the Church's fertility teaching to a tee, it was time for something else." I knew in my gut that wasn't possible for either my husband or me. We believed in the Church's teaching on contraception and dissent wasn't possible. I considered a marriage of life-long abstinence, but that wasn't what the Church wanted for our marriage either.

Humanae Vitae

In late July 1968, Pope Paul VI penned what he knew would be a critical papal document in response to contraception, abortion, and the mission of "responsible parenthood" for the faithful. The pope carefully chose each word of his encyclical letter "On the Regulation of Birth," foreseeing that "this teaching will perhaps not be easily received by all: Too numerous are those voices—amplified by the modern means of propaganda—which are contrary to the voice of the Church."[355]

---

[355]   Pope Paul VI, Of Human Life *Humanae Vitae*, July 25, 1968.

Many religious denominations had already followed the lead of the American Rabbis, Methodist Church, and Unitarians, who all sanctioned contraception. But, as Margaret Sanger had said, "the Bishops at Lambeth gave us one of our greatest triumphs by voting 193 to 67 in favor of birth control."[356] The Anglican bishops voted in 1930 at the Lambeth Conference and resolved that "in those cases where there is such a clearly felt moral obligation to limit or avoid parenthood, and where there is a morally sound reason for avoiding complete abstinence, the Conference agrees that other methods may be used."[357]

The only one left to fall to the demands of popular culture decades later was the kingpin, and America awaited a papal statement that was in line with progressive church leaders. Many held Margaret Sanger's previously exposed belief: "In spite of Church canons [Catholics] were using contraceptives, and the Church, in its wisdom, was obliged to change the law to keep its parishioners from breaking it."[358] Sanger and others refused to recognize that no commandment would still stand if the Church changed each one to prevent her parishioners from breaking God's law.

Single, young Americans who were fully saturated in the free-love mentality of the Sexual Revolution revolted against the Catholic Church's rejection of contraception as archaic and irrelevant. Many married Catholics were also disobedient to Church teachings on contraception. Americans relied on secular media outlets to translate Catholic teaching

---

356 Sanger, *The Autobiography of Margaret Sanger*, 411.
357 The Lambeth Conference, Resolution 15, 1930.
358 Sanger, *The Autobiography of Margaret Sanger*, 411.

for them, which were persuasively biased. The pope's worst opposition however came from within the Church. A faction of Catholic priests and bishops threatened to band together in dissent from the pope if he refused to conform to the modern teaching on birth control. Paul VI seemed to be isolated and alone—a single man with religious authority who seemingly knew nothing of the realities of married life and the physical, mental, and economic burdens that continuous childbearing heaped on the shoulders of the family.

America was horrified by Pope Paul VI's response to their demands. He admitted his powerlessness to alter Gospel truths as well as natural law and infallible Church doctrine. The pope refused to submit the bride of Christ to be buffeted by the torrents of the social currents of contraception, abortion, and eugenics. People were not surprised at the pope's exclusion of abortion from among the licit means of regulating birth, but they didn't expect the equal exclusion of voluntary sterilization and artificial birth control. But Paul VI firmly denied these means even "if, thereby, we secure the harmony and peace of the family, and better conditions for the education of the children already born."[359]

He was accused of ignorance and bigotry and called a dogmatist. The pope was believed to be "harking back to the Dark Ages," as Margaret Sanger had once accused. Despite having died two years before *Humanae Vitae*, Sanger's birth control arguments against the Catholic Church were resurrected, which accused the Church of using the "same arguments that had been used to hinder every advance in our

---

[359]   Pope Paul VI, On Human Life *Humanae Vitae*, July 25, 1968.

civilization—that it was against nature, against God, against the Bible, against the country's best interests, and against morality."[360] But Pope Paul VI taught that only God was the author of truth and nature and the hearts of men. He was safeguarding and interpreting those unchangeable truths.

The pope's first assertion was that the transmission of human life was a "most serious duty." It was reserved *only* for married people who became "the free and responsible collaborators with God the Creator." Paul VI declared that sex was exclusive to marriage in honoring the sacredness of human life and the inherent dignity of each child, saying in his encyclical letter that it was "right and just" for children to be born into a family. The pope was aware of scientific advances and the changing roles of women in society. He was also greatly familiar with the notion of "responsible parenthood." However, the pope and American society differed drastically on that definition.

Pope Paul VI possessed the vision of men and women in totality, not accidental and temporal, but endowed with natural (earthly) and supernatural (eternal) vocations. He believed men and women were created with the desire to make a reciprocal gift of themselves and to be in communion with others, as God communes with them. Pope Paul VI regarded marriage to be "the wise institution of the Creator to realize in mankind His design of love."[361] Baptized men and women didn't approach marriage as a sign of submission to institutionalized protocols. Rather, the sacramental

---

360   Sanger, *The Autobiography of Margaret Sanger*, 421.
361   *Humanae Vitae*.

sign of grace elevated them to become representatives of the union shared by Christ and his Church.

Pope Paul VI's encyclical *Humanae Vitae* emphasized the magnanimous holy union of marriage. He taught that marriage was far beyond our instinct and nature. It required a free and enduring act of the will, a total gift of ourselves, faithfulness and exclusivity until death, and it must be ordered toward "begetting and educating" children, who are "the supreme gift of marriage." Paul VI recognized the life-altering phenomenon parents encounter when they have children, which is not without sacrifices—sometimes heroic sacrifices. But he reminded Christians to sanctify those sacrifices in directing them toward God and to be inspired by divine love. Pope Paul VI explained the incompatibility of abortion and the artificial regulation of birth with the selfless motivation to emulate Christ in marriage.

Union and Procreation

The Trinity displays a perfect communion of love, which is always in union and always bringing forth new life. But flawed men and women in imperfect marriages struggle to reflect this love. We want an answer to relieve our struggle of being overburdened with mental, physical, and economic pressures. Catholics wondered if Pope Paul VI was out of touch and if his teaching in *Humanae Vitae* posed a threat to married love. They questioned the union of their married love that was being challenged by periods of physical separation in order to avoid procreation.

But Paul VI was not sanctioning endless parenthood at will. Rather, husbands and wives must "recognize fully their own duties towards God, towards themselves, towards the family and towards society, in a correct hierarchy of values."[362] God's generosity, which perhaps seems foolish and reckless in the total giving of himself, is the model of married couples. His generosity is the guide for large families and for families with little spacing.

Humanae Vitae was counter-cultural, but it was what the Church needed. The pope affirmed that marriage required a unique way of both husbands and wives giving themselves *totally* to their spouses and *pouring* themselves out for their children. His teaching dispelled selfishness and encouraged Catholics to be enriched by God with a special generosity, guided by prudence, in order to fulfill their gifts of self to one another.

Paul VI explained the inseparable connection of union and procreation in the marital act. He said that "every marriage act must remain open to the transmission of life." He taught that separating the conjugal act from its meaning was intrinsically disordered and unworthy of the human person, allowing for any number of exploitations. *Humanae Vitae* instructed that conjugal love must be *whole* in its act *and* meaning in order to preserve its truth as mutual love. "To use this divine gift destroying, even if only partially, its meaning and its purpose is to contradict the nature both of

---

[362]   Ibid.

man and of woman and of their most intimate relationship," the pope wrote in his encyclical.[363]

Paul VI also responded to the anticipated criticism concerning the popular topic of responsible parenthood. He wrote, "In relation to physical, economic, psychological and social conditions, responsible parenthood is exercised, either by the deliberate and generous decision to raise a numerous family, or by the decision, made for grave motives and with due respect for the moral law, to avoid for the time being, or even for an indeterminate period, a new birth."[364]

The Loophole

Years before *Humanae Vitae* was released, Margaret Sanger perceived "a loophole" in the Catholic Church's teaching on contraception. She criticized the inaccuracy and circumvented the Catholic method of being unitive while avoiding procreation without the use of contraceptives. Church teaching follows that if there are "serious motives to space out births . . . it is then licit to take into account the natural rhythms immanent in the generative functions, for the use of marriage in the [infertile] periods only, and in this way to regulate birth without offending the moral principles."[365]

Many critics believed that the Church's regulation of birth was almost equal to the Lambeth decision, which allowed Anglicans the use of contraceptives. Critics found the Church teaching to be a *natural* way of deceiving their

---

363   Ibid.
364   Ibid.
365   Ibid.

professed truth on the inseparable union of love with its meaning. Yet Paul VI was not scrambling to appease Catholics by pushing contraceptive alternatives. He was reaffirming what Pope Pius XI said in 1930 and Pope Pius XII in 1951.

Science began studying and better understanding female fertility cycles. A natural rhythm method was developed in the absence of contraceptives, which became public around 1932. Women were taught to track the rhythm of their fertility in order to discover and periodically abstain during fertile periods, when necessary, to avoid conception. Critics at the time were aghast and Margaret Sanger accused, in her 1938 autobiography, that "apparently the only distinction in the pros and cons of the birth control question was that the method we advocated was a scientific one under supervision of doctors; that of the Catholics had not been proved scientifically."[366] Birth control advocates scoffed at the unscientific "Catholic birth control," which they viewed as a desperate development in order for Catholics to have their cake and eat it too. Society applauded the chemical experimentation of birth control over working with God and nature.

But as the rhythm method developed into more scientifically accurate methods, which utilized basal body temperature and tracked hormones through blood, urine, and vaginal mucus, women began to experience a new liberation. Women who were following these "counter-cultural" methods were equipped with a deeper understanding of their fertile cycles and often recognized the symptoms of hormonal

---

[366]   Sanger, *The Autobiography of Margaret Sanger*, 426.

imbalances and serious underlying conditions. As harmful side effects of birth control were also exposed, secularists as well as infertile couples became interested in these natural methods to pinpoint their fertile windows.

Catholics, however, remained divided from secularists in their *purpose* for pursuing these natural methods. As Pope Paul VI reminded us, contracepting and non-contracepting couples may both be avoiding children for plausible reasons, but the contracepting couples "impede the development of natural process," while the non-contracepting couples "make legitimate use of a natural disposition." The pope recognized that the non-contracepting couples are called to a greater sacrifice in abstaining during periods of heightened sexual desirability. Sanger had previously criticized this as well, asking, "What could be more unnatural than to restrict intercourse to the very time when nature had least intended it?"[367]

Pope Pius XII clarified the Church's teaching on this in his 1951 *Address to Midwives on the Nature of Their Profession,* stating that entering into a marriage with the intention of limiting union *solely* to sterile periods was invalid.[368] The Catholic Church has always professed the importance of conjugal love in marriage, which is cultivated through a delicate balance in the lifelong love of the couple. Modern Catholics face a new temptation as scientific developments have almost replaced contraception with accurate methods for tracking and avoiding openness to life. My husband and

---

[367]   Ibid., 412.
[368]   Pope Pius XII, *Address to Midwives on the Nature of Their Profession,* 1951.

I faced this when we discovered an extremely accurate phone app, developed by Swiss physicists, which input my basal body temperature into a perfect algorithm and seemingly mastered our fertility. For this reason, Catholics need to guard against the temptation to lean on these natural methods as "birth control" for selfish reasons.

Pope Pius XII also addressed serious instances requiring women to avoid pregnancy in marriage. He said that the Church's position on abstaining in marriage would be troubling: "It will be objected that such an abstention is impossible, that such a heroism is asking too much." Still, the Church rejected contraception and judged that men and women were capable of continuous heroism with the help of God. Pius XII quoted St. Augustine in writing, "God does not command the impossible but while He commands, He warns you to do what you can and to ask for the grace for what you cannot do and He helps you so that you may be able."[369]

Consequences

When men and women deny their act of love its procreative right, far from avoiding the consequence of new life, they dismantle their act of love, according to Catholic philosopher Maria Fedoryka in *Only Union Plus Fruit Equals Love*[370] Men and women were given the use of *reason* and *will* in order to rule their passions instead of becoming slaves

---

[369]   Ibid.

[370]   Maria Fedoryka, *Only Union Plus Fruit Equals Love, Why Humanae Vitae Is Still Right* (San Francisco: Ignatius Press, 2016), 191.

to their passions. We must apply this to openness to life in marriage regardless of how advanced and "safe" our methods of regulating and transmitting life become. After all, our distinct ability to control our passions separates us from the animals and maintains laws against rape and sexual abuse.

Pope Paul VI's warnings against the use of artificial birth control in *Humanae Vitae* seemed exaggerated and ridiculous to many. He predicted that infidelity would increase in our culture, along with a general lowering of morality. He said that men would lose respect for women "to the point of considering her as a mere instrument of selfish enjoyment." The pope even suggested the danger of public authorities using sterilizations and governments eugenically "imposing upon their peoples, if they were to consider it necessary."[371] His arguments seemed to be imbued with fear and to discredit science, which was quickly surpassing the limits of man's domination over his body.

Many feminists stood by the fallacy that "the ends justify the means" when it comes to sex. Feminists became convinced that it was impossible for a woman to be "used" if she was also "using" the other person, as evidenced by Helen Gurley Brown and *Cosmo*. They held the argument that sex could have a mutual benefit without harm to either person if it wasn't intended to be an act of love. The Church rejected this, and while recognizing that sex produced mutual pleasure, the Church denied that a person's intent could change the meaning of sex. Pope St. John Paul II explained in *Love and Responsibility*, written in 1981, that when two people

---

[371]   *Humanae Vitae.*

purposely avoid love while engaging in the most unifying act of love, and confess to be "using" each other, they discover the "antithesis of love."[372] He taught that in "using" another person, we deny the inherent dignity and purpose of that person. Ultimately, when exercising this utilitarian approach to another human being, we offend love and harm our own soul.

Science has proven the natural release of bonding chemicals in the brain during sex. The Church has simultaneously upheld the teaching that human beings are a union of body and soul. Therefore, a woman who is pregnant experiences the physical, mental, and spiritual aspects of bringing forth that new life. She does not experience pregnancy solely in her body, because her soul is equally present in all acts of her body. She cannot turn off the chemicals in her brain or separate her soul from her body. According to the Catholic theologian Donald P. Asci, a woman's experience of this truth in sex, or the lack of her experience, cannot alter its truth and meaning; they are objective and not based on her subjective experience.[373]

Pope Paul VI's tragic predictions in *Humanae Vitae* have come to fruition in the most dreadful ways in America and abroad. Contraception has become the most reliable source of avoiding pregnancy despite exposing its eugenic origin. Margaret Sanger's condemned practice of abortion

---

[372]   Pope John Paul II, *Love and Responsibility* (San Francisco: Ignatius Press, 1981), 33.

[373]   Donald P. Asci, "Conjugal Chastity and the Procreative Personalism of Pope John Paul II," *Josephinum Journal of Theology*, vol. 14, no.2, 2007, 203.

has become an empire under Planned Parenthood. The exploitation of human beings through infidelity, pornography, and human trafficking are innumerable. And yet contraception remains a measure of progress which frees us from self-mastery.

Most of the world was deaf to Pope Paul VI's profession that "this discipline [of periodic abstinence] which is proper to the purity of married couples, far from harming conjugal love, rather confers on it a higher human value."[374] Contracepting married couples refused this assertion, believing that it was *impossible* for them to offend one another by using contraception with the intent of preserving their existing family's state of tranquility. These contracepting married couples, having already experienced motherhood and fatherhood, intentionally shut off their love from its creative cooperation with God (present even in infertile couples and after menopause naturally makes procreation impossible). As explained by Dr. Asci, the greater the love, the greater the chastity that is required. He explained that when contraception takes the place of chastity in marriage and the couple is free to disregard the woman's natural fertility cycles, the relationship exists under the constant shadow of concupiscence, which always threatens to transform it into a process of mutual use.[375]

When we justify the ends with the means in sex, we convince ourselves that love *is* our intention for disobedience. But love cannot belong to disobedience and humanity is

---

[374]   *Humanae Vitae.*

[375]   Asci, "Conjugal Chastity and the Procreative Personalism of Pope John Paul II," 189.

incapable of rewriting truth. Children of a fruitful marriage, which is obedient to truth, learn by example to reject utilitarian approaches. They are ingrained with a "just appraisal of human values," which directs their sacrifices to be equally heroic.[376]

Extremes

Catholic dogma harbors no "loopholes" or "exceptions." The Church, however, affirms the principle of totality in facing extreme medical cases. Pope Pius XII defined the principle of totality in his 1952 address on *The Moral Limits of Medical Research And Treatment,* saying that "the patient can allow individual parts to be destroyed or mutilated when and to the extent necessary for the good of his being as a whole."[377] The pope's focus remained on the *intent* of the surgical procedure, which can never have a primary focus on destroying or preventing life. The principle of totality focuses on the person as a whole. Life that is destroyed in the process of preserving the patient must remain an *unintended* "side effect" of the process.

For example, in the case of a pregnant woman with uterine cancer, the doctor may remove the uterus to save the woman's life. Although the inadvertent result of the surgery is the baby's death, the intent is not abortion and is, therefore, licit. The Church ultimately leaves the decision to each person. St. Gianna Beretta Molla, who was a physician

---

[376]   *Humanae Vitae.*
[377]   Pius XII, *The Moral Limits of Medical Research And Treatment,* September 14, 1952.

herself, exemplified heroic sacrifice on this front: she cooperated in pregnancy with having a uterine tumor removed but opted against the recommended abortion or hysterectomy in order to preserve the life of her daughter. While the surgery was successful, further complications cost Gianna her life. She is the patron saint of mothers, unborn children, and physicians.

The Catholic Church seeks the preservation of human life in all circumstances. The Church always considers the individual as an undivided whole and is personal in her approach. She is guided by truth and love, and each moral situation is ordered as such.

The Power of Masculine Virtue

"Christ . . . assigns the dignity of every woman as a task to every man; at the same time he assigns also the dignity of every man to every woman."[378]

—St. John Paul II

My father is a hero of epic proportions and I love him dearly. He climbed his way out of a childhood filled with episodes of poverty and abuse and took pride in breaking those chains. He became the first in his family not only to attend college but also to complete a Master's program at Johns Hopkins University. As he rose through the ranks of the police force and led a SWAT team, my brother and I gained ample bragging rights. We were quick to show off magazine pictures of him rappelling from helicopters and nightly news interviews of him at crime scenes after shootouts. My dad is a real-life GI Joe with a shockingly funny wit and a sentimental heart that has remained true to his high school sweetheart, my mother.

My father was out doing daily drug raids and locking up kids not much older than me for drugs and prostitution

---

[378]   John Paul II, *Man and Woman He Created Them* (Boston: Pauline Books & Media, 2006), 519.

while I was in high school. His heart would ache for the girls who were selling their bodies for twenty dollars' worth of crack, and he would wonder where their fathers were. But as my rebellious heart hardened in my early teens, I didn't notice any of the crosses my dad was carrying. I couldn't understand why I was encountering the equally hard heart of my once sacrificial father. I began to resent his stifled expressions of love and impossibly high bar, which kept an imaginary distance between us.

I began digging in the arsenal of unhealthy defense mechanisms as a response to my emotions. This resulted in screaming and door-slamming and the intentional avoiding of my parents, which allowed us to exist in the same house for weeks without exchanging more than verbal necessities.

My anger prevailed in that silence. It festered and rotted and spawned new ideas of betrayal and being unloved. I began lying even when I didn't have to, sneaking out of the house at night, and on one occasion, I ran away from home. I had somehow become a disappointment to my father—the man who was once everything to me—and I was sure that he felt like a disappointment to me as well.

I'll never forget one disrespectful fight that I had with my parents before walking out, which ended in a call from my dad telling me to come home and get all of my belongings before the trash service picked them up that week. When I got to the house, I found absolutely everything I owned tossed out in the front yard. Scattered clothes had been dumped from drawers, posters ripped from walls, and even my alarmed bunny in her disheveled cage was among my outcast belongings. I didn't have to ask; I knew what it meant. I was being evicted, kicked out of the house that my teenage angst had brought so much misery down upon.

"How did I get here," I fumed as I furiously stuffed my belongings into my friend's car and drove away, defeated. As I sat in tears, eating spaghetti on her couch, I knew that I faced a seemingly impossible uphill climb to regain my parents' trust and repair our relationship. My dad ended a heated conversation that evening with my friend's mom, and for the next few weeks, I lived at their house.

Fr. Lawrence Lovasik wrote in his 1962 *Catholic Family Handbook* that "fatherhood is a vocation in God's service, to be held . . . with the serious determination of a serious man."[379] My dad was nothing if not serious about his fatherhood, and I'm grateful for that. I moved back home a few weeks later and realized how good it was to be back under the same roof as my brother. We all knew that our previous family drama was only loosely buried under a neutral atmosphere, and none of us truly desired to continue living that way. But our hunger for a deep and meaningful family relationship seemed to have missed its time, destined to forever remain a wound. One of the first miracles God worked in me was the healing of that relationship: the anger, resentment, and the use of unhealthy defense mechanisms, which I had grown dependent upon.

You'll soon learn how the following years brought me back to religion and convinced me that humility was a necessary part of love. I had to approach my parents with love

---

[379]   Lawrence George Lovasik, *The Catholic Family Handbook* (New Hampshire: Sophia Institute Press, 1962), 15.

regardless of our past wrongs. Love was a choice, and I was choosing charity instead of hostility. The first time that I returned home from the security of college wasn't easy. I felt like a baby bird leaving its newfound nest and as I encountered my old friends and past surroundings, I prayed to retain the peace that Christ had promised.

To my surprise, my parents didn't reject my radical change in Christ, and although the process was slow, my relationship with them was eventually healed. That seemingly insurmountable obstacle to my faith—namely, unforgiveness—was annihilated. Through that process, my parents showed support as I wholeheartedly embraced Catholicism, and their initial curiosity gave way to a certain openness, which ultimately led to their complete transformation of heart as well. We were free!

So many happy family memories have since been made through our obedience to the Christian example. The hurts of the past now seem distant and faded. When I think of my parents, my mind plays the images of their smiles. I think of us dancing at my wedding. I think of announcing to them that their first grandchild would be a boy—the first of several grandchildren who adore them. The wounds that we've inflicted and the wounds that we bear may not be reconciled as easily as mine were with my parents. But most of our wounds can be healed and forgiven, setting us captives free. Christ is the divine physician, and as Scripture reminds us, "The Lord will fight for you, and you have only to be still."[380]

---

[380]   Exodus 14:14.

Toxic Masculinity and Effeminacy

Living in Washington, DC, in my late twenties put me in a great position to meet people, but many of the men I came across were doing the bare minimum to get by. They displayed no incentive to improve in any area of their lives. These men weren't seriously pursuing any of the wonderful young women surrounding them, because they refused to put forth the effort that a relationship demanded and they feared risking rejection. They had grown comfortable in their socially explosive bachelor lifestyles. It was off-putting to encounter these same men year after year at events.

When I met my husband, he stood in stark contrast to these men. He had worked hard to secure his engineering job, had his own apartment, and was decisive in what he wanted. He was also humble and self-aware enough to be constantly bettering himself. We became fast friends, and when I first turned him down as a boyfriend, he didn't wilt or resent me. Instead, he remained fervent and true as a friend until he won me over. Our first real date was a big deal to him, and not knowing which option I would choose, he planned both a picnic and made backup reservations at a fancy restaurant (we went there!). My love, respect, and admiration for him has grown in tandem, and he continues to excel in virtue as a man, a husband, and a father.

Feminism has had a hard time coexisting with masculinity—a term often prefaced with "toxic." While some strands of feminism have revolted against male behaviors promoting violence, sex, status, and aggression as measurements of strength and success, others have adopted and even exploited these unhealthy behaviors. Many modern psychologists have taken the approach of Simone de Beauvoir in determining that there is *not* and never has *been* such a thing as "masculinity." According to them, a male is merely distinct in body parts and chemistry, while any behaviors associated with being "male" are the product of social constructs.

Masculinity poses a modern cultural crisis. When masculinity is stripped from being biological, inevitable, or even stable, it rejects the reality of its universal and God-given masculine virtues. Instead, masculinity becomes interpreted as perpetual power passed through patriarchal favoritism. Society's portrait of masculine *toxicity* goes far beyond the detestable image of a violent abuser or a lecherous man undressing women with his eyes and gesturing obscenely. The modern definition challenges the existence of any virtue or value distinct to masculinity. It sees mankind as one indistinct emotional being without innate and separate virtues of excellence. Even without the example of Christ, this is impossible. Still, the modern characteristics of traditional— now termed "toxic" (hegemonic)—masculinity are *emotional stoicism, homophobia, not showing vulnerability, self-reliance, and competitiveness.*[381]

But there was a traditional characteristic of masculinity that almost every culture originally regarded as toxic: effeminacy. Although effeminacy is modernly translated as displaying "feminine" qualities, in ancient Greece, effeminacy (*malakia*) was better described as cowardice produced by

---

[381]   *APA Guidelines for Psychological Practice with Boys and Men*, August 2019, 11.

moral weakness. Aristotle, possessing a much better grasp of masculinity than what he believed to be its "defective" feminine counterpart, defined the effeminate man as self-indulgent and yielding easily to excessive pleasure. The effeminate man, lacking morals or self-control, was extravagant in essential bodily pleasures such as food, sleep, and comfort, even when these were opposed to his reason. The temperate (manly) man, on the other hand, was strong-minded in overcoming overindulgent pleasures and patient, as well as long-suffering in overcoming pain. Aristotle recognized that "in most cases men are neither much-enduring nor effeminate but midway, though inclining rather to what is worse."[382]

St. Thomas Aquinas elevated Aristotle's teaching through the illumination of faith. In Scripture, effeminacy is associated with the unjust (1 Cor 6:10), male cult prostitutes (Hos 4:14; 1 Kgs 14:24), extreme sloth (Prv 18:8), or a baseness without the honor of counsel, judgement, or prophesy (Is 3:4).[383] Aquinas said that the effeminate man was "ready to forsake a good on account of difficulties," while the persevering man "does not forsake a good on account of long endurance of difficulties and toil."[384] Whether his effeminacy was due to an unnatural vice (masturbation, sodomy, pornography), a frail temperament, or having grown too accustomed to pleasure, the effeminate man was opposed to work and consumed by leisure and relaxation. American philosopher

---

[382]   Walter Mooney Hatch, *The Moral Philosophy of Aristotle* (London: Bradbury, Agnew, & Co., 1879), 392.

[383]   Douay-Rheims Bible.

[384]   Thomas Aquinas, *Summa Theologica* II-II, q. 138, a. 1.

Kristin Popik argued that although Aquinas inherited Aristotle's belief in woman's "natural inferiority, [Aquinas differed in his belief that] the woman is equally human as the man." Accordingly, women would rise in perfection as women and not as men.[385]

These philosophers of old, who measured all things in relation to virtue, certainly didn't describe masculinity as we've come to understand it today: power, wealth, body-building, big screen TVs, and all things related to grilling. True masculinity had a lot less to do with externals and a lot more to do with internal self-formation. Aristotle and Aquinas taught that a man should measure himself by his virtue in pursuing what's good, even when it doesn't come easily. Men should find a degree of fulfillment in their work, temper their pleasure, and strive to suffer patiently when overcoming pain.

The effeminate man who is ruled by fear and pleasure is an example of masculine vice—too comfortable or afraid to pursue what he knows is good for himself, his family, or his greater purpose in life due to the difficult challenges or rigorous work required. Effeminate men also display moral weakness in yielding to non-essential pleasures such as fame, wealth, and honor, even when these are destructive to their soul and neither serve others nor glorify God.

Today, we commonly joke about men addicted to the entertainment culture—whether living in their parent's basements playing video games, avoiding marriage and responsibility, or leaving all the tough family decisions to their wives.

---

[385]   Kristin M. Popik, *The Philosophy of Woman of St. Thomas Aquinas* (Christendom College Press, 1978).

These men complain rather than taking decisive action geared toward change and allow their emotions to master their hearts. Effeminate men desire passivity over engagement in decision-making and conflict resolution. They are averse to challenging mental and physical activity and allow themselves to grow weak in character and will. According to Aristotle and Aquinas, effeminate men are inclined to wealth and leisure and avoid any risk on the path of excellence in pursuing the good.

Modern Knights

Pope Pius XI's 1935 encyclical on the Catholic priesthood stated, "Most of the saintly bishops and priests whose 'praise the Church declares,' owe the beginning of their vocation and their holiness to example and teaching of a father strong in faith and manly virtues, of a pure and devoted mother, and of a family in which the love of God and neighbor, joined with simplicity of life, has reigned supreme."[386] As of 2019, about seven million fathers were completely "absent" from the lives of their minor children according to a US Census Bureau article.[387] Aside from putting their children at greater risk of poverty, behavioral disorders, and legal detention, physically and emotionally absent fathers also rob their children of a proper male example. Since childhood learning is largely built upon modeled behavior, children without a male role model often look to peers, celebrities, or

---

[386]   Pope Pius XI, *Ad Catholici Sacerdotii*, December 20, 1935.
[387]   Lindsay M. Monte, "'Solo' Dads and 'Absent' Dads Not as Different as They Seem," November 05, 2019.

other adult males (who don't always have their best interests at heart).

With or without a *present* father, all boys will eventually face the "blessing and dilemma" to "be a man." Author Robert Lewis reflected on how fathers were handicapping their sons from "knowing how to move out of childhood into manhood." Lewis said this was happening by the failure of fathers to deliver a "biblically grounded *definition of manhood*" to their sons. He also drew attention to the lack of teachable moments in embracing manhood and the "loss of *ceremony*" marking a boy's passage into manhood.[388] According to Lewis, young men are left with confusion around what true masculinity *is* or *should* be, so they instead cling to success, prestige, aggression, or "toughness" as their measurements of manliness, or reject masculinity all together, recoiling from anything deemed "masculine."[389]

Masculinity has also been defined by chivalry. When we hear the term "chivalry" today, we might think of a man opening a door for a woman or pushing in her chair. But the term originally meant the righteous code of conduct of the medieval knight, who was guided by his Christian faith. The ideals of chivalry were born in the eleventh and twelfth centuries with the crusades—requiring *belief and observation of all the Church teaches, defending the Church, respecting and defending the weak, loving your country of birth, not recoiling before an enemy, declaring merciless war on the Infidel,*

---

[388]   Robert Lewis, *Raising a Modern-Day Knight, A Father's Role in Guiding His Son to Authentic Manhood* (Illinois: Tyndale House Publishers, Carol Stream, 1997), 16.

[389]   Ibid.

scrupulously performing feudal duties, never lying or being unfaithful to a pledged word, giving generously to others, and always being the champion of the right and the good against injustice and evil.[390] When a nation became "effeminate"—decadent, tyrannical, and oppressive—medieval knights believed God made use of them to chastise the corrupt, wrote nineteenth-century French historian Léon Gautier.[391]

Knighthood was a rigorous religious process requiring herculean effort and monastic discipline. The knight's chivalric code of defending goodness against injustice and evil were socially adopted throughout the ages and became famously promoted in the works of nineteenth-century American author Howard Pyle and the Arthurian legends (in which only Sir Galahad perfectly upheld the code of conduct). Arthur's fictitious knights swore an additional protection of feminine virtue at their annual Pentecostal oath (occurring on Pentecost). They swore to strengthen ladies, damsels, gentlewomen, and widows "in their rights, and never to enforce them." A knight who violated this oath did so "upon pain of death."[392] The misuse of knightly service was a mortal offense, often portrayed by the character Gawain, who according to the *Handbook of Arthurian Romance*, "is the embodiment of the undisciplined knight, the warrior whose

---

390   Léon Gautier, *Chivalry* (London: George Routledge and Sons, 1891), 26.
391   Ibid., 3.
392   Sir. Thomas Malory, *Le Morte Darthur: The Pentecostal Oath*, Book III, Chapter XV.

uncontrolled and unrestrained action leads to conflict, misfortune and death of innocents."[393]

True Masculinity

These noble hallmarks of chivalry—honor, honesty, valor, and loyalty—when elevated with a *transcendent cause* that is truly heroic, timeless, and supremely meaningful, give answer to the question of *who* a man is rather than *what* he does, Lewis wrote in *Raising a Modern-Day Knight*.[394] This vision integrates a man's life and connects him in time and eternity with Christ, who is the perfection of masculinity. True masculinity models Jesus's self-donating love and, through it, discovers excellence of virtue. It is impossible to think of masculinity apart from Christ. Men and women are sanctified in body and soul through Christ, and their dignity is rooted and perfected in him. "Whoever follows after Christ, the perfect man, becomes himself more of a man," Pope Paul VI wrote in his 1965 encyclical on the Church in the modern world.[395]

When Father Francis Lasance wrote *The Young Man's Guide* in 1910, he stated that nothing was more honorable than serving God. He instructed that masculine piety exists when a man's will is "employed in its full strength for God's honor and glory, in His holy service."[396] Father

---

[393] Leah Tether and Johnny McFadyen, *Handbook of Arthurian Romance* (Berlin: De Gruyter, 2017), 15.

[394] Lewis, 68.

[395] Pope Paul VI, On the Church in the Modern World *Gaudium et Spes* (December 7, 1965), no. 42.

[396] Francis X. Lasance, *The Young Man's Guide* (Illinois: St. Augustine

Lasance taught that the character of a man who is wholly righteous and submits to God's will is rooted in self-control, moral courage, and a firm determination to do what is right because it is pleasing to God, not the world. Lasance revealed a model of Christian masculinity for young men in danger of becoming the "inglorious victim of vanity, selfishness, and human respect" at the cost of abandoning their beliefs and molding themselves into many shameful forms. Father Lasance wrote that the virtue of the Christian man is the pearl of his character, politeness is born of his self-denial, and cheerfulness is his potent influence for good. Kindness is the Christian man's habitual disposition of heart, and he is always ready to defend, with gentleness and reverence, the hope that is within him.[397]

Jesus is the antithesis of *anything* toxic existing in masculinity. Concerning *emotional stoicism*: Jesus was so moved by Mary and the Jews mourning the death of Lazarus that he also wept. However, Jesus didn't raise Lazarus from the dead as an emotional response; he did so to glorify God.[398] Regarding *homophobia*: Jesus expressed love of sinners and hatred of sin. He said in the Gospel of Matthew, "It is better that you lose one of your members than that your whole body go into hell."[399] Jesus also emphasized the need for showing mercy to a neighbor, even when it challenges one's identity

Academy Press, 2012), 341.

[397]   1 Peter 3:15.

[398]   John 11:32–40.

[399]   Matthew 5:30.

and tribal loyalties, as in the story of the Good Samaritan in Luke's Gospel.[400]

Jesus didn't *compete* with the Pharisees, although he challenged their rules and standard of authority when he healed and cast out demons on the Sabbath. Knowing the hearts of the Pharisees, Jesus shamed them and called them "hypocrites" in the synagogue.[401] Jesus was also not *self-reliant*, living thirty of his earthly years obediently with his parents and never acting outside the Father's will. We see him several times in the Gospels retreating to a quiet place to pray and refuel on the Father's unifying love and strength rather than trying to soldier through on his own reserves. Jesus also chose twelve apostles to accompany him and carry out his earthly work after his resurrection.

Jesus *showed vulnerability* but was always spiritually guarded, demonstrating both human fragility and supernatural strength in agonizingly sweating blood, falling under the weight of the cross on the road to Calvary, and embracing the passionate work of redemption from the humble state of one who was tortured and accused. This is the authentic model of masculinity, masculine piety, and sacrificial masculine love.

Christ is our ideal, and as Archbishop Fulton Sheen wrote in his 1953 book *Life Is Worth Living*, "The higher the love, the more demands will be made on us to conform to that ideal."[402] In other words, the height of Christ's love is

---

[400] Luke 10:33.

[401] Luke 13:10–17.

[402] Fulton Sheen, *Life Is Worth Living* (San Francisco: Ignatius Press, 1999).

infinite, and Christianity demands much of us in conforming to that ideal. Masculinity can't be dissolved or rewritten because its ideal is forever perfected in Christ. Christians also can't settle for less or pretend that we don't want more. I glimpsed this in the stark difference between my husband's character and the other slothful men surrounding me, as my future husband strived to "be worthy" of the same noble character he saw in me.

Women responding to masculinity cannot do so by transforming their femininity to become the worst of masculinity, demonstrating dominating and aggressive traits. Women also can't make up for what men may be lacking in their masculinity. Women must respond by achieving the highest ideal of their femininity. As Fulton Sheen so eloquently wrote, "When a man loves a woman, he has to become worthy of her. The higher her virtue, the more noble her character, the more devoted she is to truth, justice, goodness, the more a man has to aspire to be worthy of her."[403] American abolitionist Wendell Phillips observed in the nineteenth century, "Social science affirms that woman's place in society marks the level of civilization."[404] Sheen elevated this in the twentieth century, saying, "The history of civilization could actually be written in terms of the *level* of its women."

---

[403] Ibid.
[404] Wendall Phillips, *The Phrenological Journal and Science of Health: 1881*, vol. 73-75 (New York: Fowler & Wells), 241.

PART THREE

The Dignity of Women

A New Beginning

"The dignity of women is measured by the order of love, which is essentially the order of justice and charity."[405]

—St. John Paul II

The years of band practices, shows, traveling, and recording wore on me. As much as I loved the music, the band, and the crowds, something was missing. Our original bass player was addicted to heroin, another was in a mental institution, and the most recent one ditched us in Europe after playing a riot grrrl festival in Scotland. I longed for consistency even as it became increasingly harder to find. We headed into the studio to record a second album while simultaneously negotiating future tours and record contracts, but my momentum plateaued. A comical moment occurred in the studio as I belted out one haunting lyric after the other, which unknowingly exposed my growing existential search for meaning: *"When we reach the edge of this life, things will seem so much clearer to us."* Our drummer froze. I'll never forget the look on her face as she stopped,

---

[405] John Paul II, Apostolic Letter *Mulieris Dignitatem* (1988), no. 29.

wide-eyed, after several songs, and soberly asked, "We're not becoming a Christian band, are we?"

I was appalled. "Of course not!" But then again, why were so *many* of my lyrics cloaked in a thin veil of faith? I had searched for God in Wiccan bookstores and at Protestant alter calls, vowing never to look back to Catholicism. My friends accepted my philosophical introspection as the haunting facet of writer-musicians, which kept me prolific. My agnostic boyfriend recognized something deeper. He had been working at a graphic design firm owned by an Italian family. His jovial boss, Charles, often spoke about Catholicism with prophetic confidence. My boyfriend knew that I'd be fascinated by Charles, and he arranged a meeting.

I was admittedly tired of arguing with people who couldn't hold their own in a debate. I had experienced many cultures and religions and couldn't imagine returning to someone in the heart of my little hometown for such weighty answers. It seemed like an easy win for me. Dressed in black and pushing locks of bright pink hair out of my face, I strode into Charles's office with a pretentiously pharisaical attitude. I was determined to blow the roof off what he "thought" he knew. Charles greeted me with a smile that never faltered, and the familial charm of his Italian enthusiasm quickly disarmed my stoic reluctance. He saw through my layers of thick eyeliner to the depths of my soul, and I felt strangely childlike in his presence.

His spiritual confidence was alarming to me, as I was unfamiliar with the saints and the gifts of the Holy Spirit. I was skeptically surprised as he consistently answered my questions right before they came out of my mouth. It became increasingly clear to me that this man was either *with* God or *against* him. He was driven by some hidden spiritual power, which became awesomely present in that office room. The Holy Spirit and the dark forces I had allowed into my soul were at war. Hot tears melted a black stream down my face as he told me how deeply I was loved by God. Slumping down in my chair, I tried to remember the last time that someone had *truly* told me I was loved without condition, simply for *being* me. I searched my heart unsuccessfully to find the knowledge that I was loved from eternity, regardless of what I had done or not done. When I left that room, I was convinced that it wasn't too late for me and that I wasn't a lost cause!

Like George Bailey in the movie *It's a Wonderful Life*, I had been given a new beginning. Walls were crashing down inside of me as Jesus cleaned house in my soul. A mysterious box arrived at my front door from my dad's friend. It was packed with books and movies on the Catholic faith, and I discovered an old copy of Bernard Ruffin's *Padre Pio: The True Story* laying on top. Curiously devouring the book, I felt the saint's stigmatized hands figuratively reach out and shake me. Padre Pio's miraculous life had a profound influence on me and encouraged my return to Catholicism.

Charles boldly proposed an open debate with me and all of my radical friends. I didn't let him down, filling the community center with feminists and anarchists and guys who had to duck to get their mohawks into the doorway. I imagined that Charles would wet himself at the sight of our motley crew, but he welcomed us just the same as if we were wearing floral jumpers. We pelted him excitedly with questions as the debate began, and his answers strongly fought our fire with fire. Some of my friends grew angry when our debate fell on hot topics and others stormed out. I watched God work through Charles amidst the storm of our relativism. For the first time, I could *see* what God was doing. I could see with unfailing clarity what was right and what was wrong, and I laughed in spite of myself because I recognized the existence of truth!

Holy (and Not So Holy) Women

"I wanted each woman to be a rebellious Vashti, not an Esther; was she to be merely a washboard with only one song, one song?"[406]

—Margaret Sanger, *Autobiography*

Feminists often cling to the biblical bad girl trifecta of Lilith, Jezebel, and Vashti as shining examples of radical feminine strength, despite the ironic disobedience and evil that enshrouded them. Simone de Beauvoir said, "In the Bible few women are noteworthy for their actions: Ruth merely found herself a husband. Esther gained the Jews' grace by kneeling before Ahasuerus, and even then she was only a docile instrument in Mordecai's hands; Judith was bolder, but she too obeyed the priests and her exploit has a dubious aftertaste: it could not be compared to the pure and shining triumph of young David."[407] Feminists often reject submission to both men and God. Margaret Sanger was inspired by Esther's predecessor, Vashti, who she considered "the first woman rebel in history." Margaret named her newspaper *The Woman Rebel* because she wanted all

---

[406]   Sanger, *The Autobiography of Margaret Sanger*, 106.
[407]   Beauvoir, *The Second Sex*, 303.

women to be a rebellious Vashti and not a "meek and gentle Esther."[408]

From Lilith to Esther

Lilith has been adopted as the first feminist, and her namesake has been used in Wiccan orders and music festivals. Lilith is said to exist within all women. But Lilith rose from Jewish folklore and Sumerian demonology (2000 BC) as an evil spirit who seduced men and sought her revenge on babies and pregnant women. Feminists often identify with the Lilith of the satirical Hebrew text of the Middle Ages, the *Alphabet of Ben Sira*, which introduced Lilith as Adam's rebellious first wife who refused to "lie beneath" Adam. Lilith boldly fled Eden in disobedience to Adam and God, accepting her banishment and curse. Feminists have sympathized with Lilith's mythical plight, relating it to the plight of women in society.

Lilith continued to appear throughout art and literature—wrapped around Michelangelo's tree of life in the Sistine chapel and poetically depicted by Dante Gabriel Rossetti—drawing men into her web before snapping their necks and strangling their hearts with her golden hair. James Joyce called Lilith the "patron of abortions" in his 1922 book *Ulysses*, and even C. S. Lewis's Narnian White Witch of the 1950s was portrayed as the demon spawn of Lilith. Yet Lilith is not found in Scripture aside from hopeful references to the demonic night hag in Isaiah 34:14.

---

[408]   Sanger, *The Autobiography of Margaret Sanger*, 106.

Jezebel, however, is very much in Scripture, and though a queen, she certainly is not one to be emulated. Her husband, King Ahab, ruled over Israel as one in a succession of evil rulers, but Ahab "did evil in the sight of the Lord above all that were before him."[409] After marrying the idolatrous Sidonian princess Jezebel, Ahab worshiped her deity and built a temple to Ba'al. He also made a cultic object/goddess called Asherah. When the prophet Elijah prophesied a drought upon Israel, Jezebel put all of the Hebrew prophets to death. Jezebel replaced the Hebrew prophets with 450 idolatrous prophets of Ba'al, and Elijah returned to challenge them. Elijah taunted the idolatrous prophets until they had exhausted their attempts to call down fire from Ba'al. Elijah then soaked the pieces of wood on his pile three times before calling down a mighty fire from God and slaying the idolatrous prophets. The drought was ended and rain came to Israel.

Jezebel was infuriated by the death of her prophets and sent a message to Elijah vowing to end his life as he had done to them. Feminists have harkened to Jezebel's powerful role, which made the great prophet Elijah flee to the wilderness in fear of her. But Jezebel's heart was hardened toward God, and although he gave her a time to repent of her immorality, as was recorded in Revelation 2:21, Jezebel refused.[410] Elijah's successor, Elisha, anointed the military commander Jehu king of Israel. Jehu was to avenge the blood of the prophets spilled by Jezebel and the sins of the house of Ahab. After

---

409   3 Kings (1 Kings) 16, Douay-Rheims.
410   Revelation 2:21.

killing Jezebel's son on account of the many harlotries and sorceries of his mother, Jehu rode to the home of Jezebel. She painted her eyes and adorned her head, knowing Jehu's intent and facing her death. At Jehu's command, Jezebel's eunuchs threw her from the window and the horses trampled her. This fulfilled the prophesy, "the dogs shall eat the flesh of Jezebel; and the corpse of Jezebel shall be as dung upon the face of the field . . . so that no one can say, This is Jezebel."[411]

Despite radical attempts to justify them, honoring women such as Jezebel *because* of their disobedience to God seems crazy in comparison to the brave and elevated biblical women who reaped goodness by their obedience. Deborah, the prophetess and judge of Israel, gave wise counsel and led Barak and ten thousand men to defeat the Canaanite army of Sisera at the Lord's command. The Lord didn't give Barak the glory of that victory but rather delivered Sisera into the hands of a woman. That woman, Jael, drove a tent peg through Sisera's temple as he slept. She won the victory over the Canaanites for Israel. The prophetess Deborah arose as "a mother in Israel," and Jael was regarded as "blessed among women."[412]

Esther was another heroic biblical woman, despite Margaret Sanger's distain for her. Esther found favor with the Persian king and became queen, although she was a Jew. This happened after the previous Persian queen, Vashti, refused the summons of the king, who desired to show off

---

[411]   2 Kings 9:36–37.
[412]   Judges 5:24, Douay-Rheims.

her exceeding beauty to those at his banquet. Heeding the council of his wise princes who feared Vashti's disobedience would set a bad precedent for all Persian women, King Ahasuerus sent Vashti to his harem, never to enter his presence again. King Ahasuerus then sought a new queen. The Lord foretold these events to Esther's adopted father, Mordecai, in a dream. The Lord revealed to Mordecai that in a day of darkness when evil threatened the Jews, a small spring would grow into a great river. That spring was Esther, who the Lord would use to save his people.

Many young virgins went into the king's chamber decked in adornments and were added to his harem as concubines. But only Esther won his love and the royal crown, putting her in position to save her people. Mordecai began to be persecuted for not worshiping the king's highest prince, Haman. Mordecai refused to worship a man on account of his religion, and Haman became determined to kill Mordecai and all Jews in the nation, "both young and old, little children, and women."[413] Mordecai petitioned Esther on behalf of their Jewish people as Haman prepared a beam to hang him.

Esther knew that anyone entering the king's inner court unsummoned would be immediately put to death. She held a three-day fast with her handmaidens and ordered Mordecai and all Jews to do the same. Invoking God on the third day, she entered the forbidden inner chamber as the king's wrath was supernaturally changed to gentleness. Esther petitioned him for her life and the lives of her people, which

---

[413]   Esther 3:13, Douay-Rheims.

were threatened by Haman. The king ordered Haman to hang on the beam he had prepared for Mordecai and elevated Mordecai to Haman's position. All Jews from India to Ethiopia were spared on that day because of Esther. A new light rose on Esther's people and many Persians converted to the God of Queen Esther.

It certainly isn't ideal by *our* standards that Esther had to compete with a harem of women belonging to a polygamous pagan king. Just as Shadrach, Meshach, and Abednego were cast into a Babylonian furnace and Daniel was thrown into the lions' den by the Medes, Esther's witness served a greater purpose: that the God of the Jews was glorified among the pagans. Salvation history is the messy love story of Israel and their God, who has guarded, directed, and protected them. He has led them through tumultuous situations in enemy lands and raised them up to show his glory and sanctify his people. Esther, Deborah, and Jael are courageous and exemplary women.

Joan of Arc

Joan of Arc is another Christian woman who has been grossly mischaracterized throughout history. Often portrayed as brazenly disobedient, Joan has become the rebellious feminist heroine who gladly dons men's armor and gallantly rides off to war. But these images do a great disservice to the saint's heroic virtues of humility and obedience. Prayer was Joan's constant companion, giving her the strength to face inhuman obstacles and endure her torturous execution while remaining faithful to a king and God who had seemingly abandoned her.

In 1893, Lord Gower dedicated his book on Joan of Arc to his mother, observing the natural conclusion that "one who loved and admired all that is good and beautiful and high-minded should have a strong feeling of admiration for the memory of Joan of Arc."[414] This simple village maiden, whose days revolved around morning Mass, was supernaturally called to "heroic love and transcendent valour" in a time when 1420s France had sunken so low as to lose almost all power and territory to England. Joan was visited by St. Michael, patron of the French army, at the age of thirteen in the summer of 1425. She was instructed by her heavenly apparitions for three years until she was guided to seek a knight named Robert de Baudricourt and reveal to him her mission to save France and crown Charles.

Joan overcame Baudricourt's resistance and obtained pardon from her disapproving parents before beginning her mission. She humbly stated, "I am not made to follow the career of a soldier; but I must go and carry out this my calling, for my Lord has appointed me to do so."[415] She adopted military attire and cut her hair short as a measure of protection for the perilous journey. Seventeen-year-old Joan was reported to have rode joyfully and fearlessly with the knights to meet the king, attending Mass three times along the way, according to Gower.

---

[414]   Lord Ronald Sutherland Gower, *Joan of Arc* (New York: Charles Scribner's Sons, 1893).

[415]   Ibid., 15.

Charles, the heir to the French throne, was known to have weak character. He tested Joan by dressing commonly and hiding among the courtiers, claiming one of them as king. Joan knew him immediately, and after revealing a great sign to Charles (confirming his legitimacy), she resided in the castle. Joan made a "chivalrous ally and firm friend" in the young Duke of Anjou. In full armor, Joan road to Tours with a dedicated military establishment including her two brothers, a priest, and three distinct flags inscribed with "Jesu and Maria" representing her mission.

Although she regarded the sword from St. Catherine's altar as a sacred weapon, Joan said she loved her banner "forty times as much as my sword!"[416] Her banners had a sacramental power among the peasantry across the countryside, who regarded Joan as an angelic savior. Her soldiers were also re-inspired to renew their Catholic devotion through Joan's example. She had a reputation of converting her soldiers to virtuous and faithful practices in place of previous bad habits, and they often attended daily Mass and confession with her. The sacraments gave Joan the confidence to continue on her mission, demanding peace from her enemies, including the King of England, and when necessary, threatening military consequences. She did all this in the names of Jesus and Mary.

Joan often worked against the resistance and cowardice of her own king, refusing to surrender Paris even when she was struck by a crossbow bolt in the thigh. She was finally ordered by Charles to leave the battle and return to the

---

[416]   Ibid., 38.

castle where she faced fault and insult. Lord Gower wrote that Joan laid down her arms and armor at the foot of an image of Mary, humbly surrendering "any further earthly victory by the aid of arms."[417] She suffered one mortification after another as she successively learned of her victorious sites being abandoned by the king and falling back into English hands. Joan was eventually granted permission to lead a small army, whose first miraculous victory caused her enemies in the castle to conspire against her.

Joan of Arc had been entirely faithful to God and to her king. Lord Gower reported that according to all written accounts, Joan displayed "traits of her sweet nature, and of that simplicity which had endeared her so deeply to the hearts of the people: a disposition no success altered, no disappointment embittered." Gower commented that "the chief charm of her character was this simplicity, her entire freedom from self-glorification . . . although not the most glorious or salient to those who are dazzled by her triumphs and extraordinary career."[418]

In the year 1430, with advanced warning from her mystical "voices," Joan was betrayed and captured by her English and Burgundian enemies. The bishops and princes who knew her conspired against her and condemned her as a sorceress and idolatress. Joan endured a hateful and abusive imprisonment and a bitter trial before being burned as a heretic by the Church she loved. Throughout Joan of Arc's mission, many great and noble men lost their souls, but

---

417   Ibid., 113.
418   Ibid., 117–18.

many lesser men and women gained theirs. Her battle cry was "*Veni Creator*" (Come, Creator Spirit), and her faithful presence challenged the moral strength and courage of those she encountered. Joan of Arc was the faithful servant of God who violated her prison oath by wearing men's clothing to protect her chastity and chose to burn rather than commit the mortal sin of denying God. *This* is where Joan of Arc's heroism lies.

Mother of God

"The Blessed Virgin Mary is born to be Mother. The supreme consolation that our Lady receives at the cross of her Son is the assurance that her vocation as Mother does not end with Christ's death. The Lord commands the world, "Behold your Mother." The Resurrection begins for Mary, and for us, with these words. The Blessed Virgin's womb remains forever fruitful. Mary leads us to Christ, but Christ leads us back to his Mother, for without Mary's maternity, Jesus would become a mere abstraction to us."[419]

Coming to a definitive crossroads between the life I had been living and the new life I found in Christ brought a weighty agony concerning my future. Receiving acceptance to the coveted fashion design program of a prestigious New York art institution, I would be remiss not to accept their offer. On the other hand, acceptance would inevitably mean planting myself deeper among the dark influences I was desperately trying to escape. With no viable options before me, other than a far-fetched suggestion by Charles to attend a university run by Franciscan friars in the middle-of-nowhere Ohio, I ran to Mary.

---

[419]   *Magnificat*, January 1, 2018, www.magnificat.com.

I didn't need convincing or explanation about Mary's intercessory role when I went to her in prayer. I knew that when I snuck away to the small church in our hometown and found myself at the foot of her image, I was kneeling at the foot of the Mother of God. I saw in Mary a strong and gentle mother whom I could trust with my life. Our rural church housed an almost life-sized statue carved of olive-wood, giving the realistic appearance of soft bronzed skin to Christ's Mother. Her gentle eyes were large and life-like, casting their gaze from under her flowing mantle and intricate brunette braid. Her posture was particularly endearing to me because her hands seemed to have a maternal reach as they stretched down toward me. They seemed to want to elevate me in embrace like a little child. I wept shamelessly before the statue of Mary in the empty church that day, laying all cares and anxieties at her feet. This produced something truly mystical.

Out of the silence of the empty church, I heard the voice of a woman saying, "Let me lift you up." The voice was so clear and tangible that I instantly swung around to face the embarrassment of my onlooker . . . but no one was there. I slowly turned back toward the statue, dumfounded and considering whether my imagination was interfering. I soberly waited but heard nothing further. This troubled me even more because the words I had heard offered no confirmation or clear direction in answer to my prayer. I was up against the clock in making a decision for my future and time was running out. Still, I resolutely surrendered myself to let Mary "lift me up," asking for the small favor of clarification.

I told no one about the experience but decided to visit the Franciscan University of Steubenville, Ohio that Charles had so strongly recommended. My parents came along although they were unconvinced that the university held any future promise for me. I silently begged for a clear sign of revelation as we drove from Maryland to Ohio. Underwhelmed, we arrived on the university grounds set rustically on a hill above the remnants of a small mining town. Still, I waited on every moment for God's revelation as our uncommonly friendly tour-guide showed us around campus. But regardless of my attempts to discover a sign or read into words spoken, God had revealed nothing.

Concluding the tour, our guide pointed out a small church replicating the one St. Francis of Assisi had built. The portiuncula chapel was a hidden treasure on campus and offered perpetual Eucharistic adoration. I was convinced that I would discover my answer there and rushed my parents excitedly toward the little stone chapel. A holy peacefulness filled the chapel, but to my dismay, no definitive answer came to me there. A disappointing ache began to grow in the recesses of my heart as my parents headed to the car for our long journey home.

As I walked out of the chapel and providentially circled around behind it, I was surprised and awed. There before me, hidden behind the chapel, was a stone grotto with a bronzed Marian statue tucked into its tall sanctuary stone wall. The hands of the statue were lifted confidently to heaven, and I heard instantly that same feminine voice saying, "Here is where I will lift you up!"

The rest is history, as they say. I returned to the car with an otherworldly smile and kept my golden silence about the experience for many years. Against the odds of a late enrollment and surprised parents and friends, I began attending the Franciscan University of Steubenville that fall—with great conviction. It was there that my life, as well as the lives of my parents, were completely changed. I gained a much-needed foundation in humility and developed a love of service over self. I remained drawn toward serving women and began working on redeeming my femininity. With a clearer view of God's mission for my life, I wanted to help others break the bonds of spiritual oppression that had oppressed me.

The Reign of Service

Susan B. Anthony said in her 1875 speech, "When the mother of Christ shall be made the true model of womanhood and motherhood, when the office of maternity shall be held sacred and the mother shall consecrate herself, as did Mary, to the one idea of bringing forth the Christ-child, then, and not till then, will the earth see a new order of men and women, prone to good rather than evil."[420] When we hear among the last tormented words of the crucified Christ to John, "*Behold your mother*," we are met with a paradox of Mary's maternity. What did her motherhood mean to our Lord and Savior—beyond initial gestation, labor, nursing, and tireless nights? What did Mary's motherhood efficaciously mean for the redemption of sinful humanity?

---

[420]   Harper, *The Life and Work of Susan B. Anthony*, vol. II, 1011.

Christ's mission wasn't won at the expense of using and discarding human beings for his purpose. He came to redeem and bring humanity to fulfillment. Christ held his mother closest to him on earth, and through love, obedience, and friendship, she remained with him for all thirty-three years of his earthly life. Mary, whom Christ made queen of heaven and earth, the redeemer of Eve and figure of the Church, has sanctified maternity. In his 1988 apostolic letter *Mulieris Dignitatem,* St. John Paul II said the central salvific event of the Word being made flesh "is realized in her and through her. . . . Mary attains a union with God that exceeds all the expectations of the human spirit."[421] The Mother of God is the example for all women.

Though she was chosen, Mary made a free choice of her will in the same way that Esther, Joan of Arc, and many holy women have done. Her role was active and required a conscious "yes" in response to God's angelic messenger. Mary became an *active* participant in the incarnation of Christ when she said, "Be it done to me according to thy word."[422] Mary's words continued to have great power in Scripture. At the mere sound of *her* voice, John the Baptist leapt in his mother's womb and Elizabeth, filled with the Holy Spirit, cried out, "Blessed art thou among women, and blessed is the fruit of thy womb."[423] Mary's words also ushered in Jesus's public ministry and his first miracle. Knowing his true nature and purpose, Mary's intimate exchange with her Son at Cana was justly profound. Mary instructed the

---

421 *Mulieris Dignitatem,* no. 3.
422 Luke 1:38, Douay-Rheims.
423 Luke 1:42, Douay-Rheims.

servants, "Do whatever he tells you."[424] Her message was the first Christian instruction in faith.

St. John Paul II said that Scripture bears witness to the human struggle of men and women in Eve and Mary, "the struggle for his or her fundamental 'yes' or 'no' to God and God's eternal plan for humanity."[425] When the pope said that Mary possessed the highest expression of the "feminine genius," he recognized that her "fullness of grace" perfected her physical (woman) and spiritual (feminine) presence in the life of Christ and humanity.

Christianity teaches that service is an act of love whereby we show honor and respect for the dignity of another person. Christ is the "Servant of the Lord" and Mary the "handmaid of the Lord" *par excellence*. Mary was united to the messianic service of her Son, who "came not to be served but to serve."[426] Mary also made a gift of herself through her maternal reign.

Previously, God had only approached men to make his covenants, as evidenced with Noah, Abraham, and Moses. But the new covenant was made through Mary, the perfect "woman" in dignity, vocation, and union with God. Mary's sincere gift of self encompassed all the richness and personal resources of femininity. Her motherhood was united to the paschal mystery, which she suffered with her Son through faith and continues to suffer with women wounded in their human or maternal dignity.[427] As G. K. Chesterton

---

[424]   John 2:5.
[425]   *Mulieris Dignitatem*, no. 3.
[426]   Matthew 20:28.
[427]   *Mulieris Dignitatem*, no. 19.

observed, we "serve a Mother who seems to grow more beautiful as new generations rise up and call her blessed."[428] This
supernatural beauty is deeper than can be perceived through
physical senses; it is the fullness of wisdom, goodness, and
union of the beloved with her Creator.

[428]   G. K. Chesterton, *The Collected Works of G. K. Chesterton II* (San
Francisco: Ignatius Press, 1986), 401.

The Christian Household

"Even so husbands should love their wives as their own
bodies. He who loves his wife loves himself. For no man ever
hates his own flesh, but nourishes and cherishes it, as Christ
does the church, because we are members of his body."

—Ephesians 5:28–30

St. Paul holds an especially hateful place for himself among feminists, with no small help from Ephesians. Paul's seemingly overt machismo raises the scornful alarm of women who feel isolated by the tone of his letters. Women are told to learn in silence and to be submissive. They are not permitted to teach or have authority over men, according to 1 Timothy 2, which is traditionally part of the Pauline corpus. "Woman" is blamed for being deceived in the Garden of Eden and becomes a *transgressor.* According to Paul, women are "saved through bearing children, if she continues in faith and love and holiness, with modesty."[429] These teachings are averse to many of the progressive advancements we currently experience in liturgical life.

But Paul also wrote in his letter to the Galatians that "there is neither male nor female; for you are all one in

---

[429]   1 Timothy 2:15.

Christ Jesus."[430] He also wrote that Christians are all "Abraham's offspring, heirs according to promise."[431] Regardless of the distinct role played by the "man" and "woman" in our "original sin," it remains a sin of humanity. *Both* were called equally into existence in the image and likeness of God. *Both* decided to dictate what was good and evil independently of God. Even nature rebelled against their sin by mingling toil with labor and pain with childbirth and death became a necessity. Sin diminishes and obscures the reflection of God in us, as St. John Paul II taught.[432]

Sin's consequence is evident in the breaking of unity between man and woman: "He shall rule over you" (Gn 3:16). But St. John Paul II showed that dominion threatens gifting ourselves to one another, and therefore "the woman cannot become the 'object' of 'domination' and male 'possession.'"[433] She is his co-subject and not an object of pleasure or exploitation. If a man offends a woman's dignity, he acts contrary to his own, and vice-versa. If a man dominates, abandons, or accuses a woman, as exemplified in the woman caught in adultery in John's Gospel, without taking responsibility for his fault, then he is guilty of offending them both. Women are also tempted to dominate men and to deform their feminine richness in combatting his sin. Sin presents both men and women with a continual temptation to rebel against the moral order. We conquer this through striving to perfect our feminine or masculine nature.

---

[430]   Galatians 3:28.
[431]   Galatians 3:29.
[432]   *Mulieris Dignitatem,* no. 9.
[433]   Ibid., no. 10.

Mulieris Dignitatem unveiled the beautiful truth that "in Christ the mutual opposition between man and woman—which is the inheritance of original sin—is essentially overcome."[434] God, who has revealed himself as a Triune communion of love, reflects this love in the natural order through the transmission of new life. As John Paul II said, "Man and woman are called from the beginning not only to exist "side by side" or "together," but they are also called to *exist mutually* "*one for the other.*"[435]

Paul used a spousal relationship in his letter to the Ephesians to describe the profound mystery of Christ and the Church. Jesus is the bridegroom, and through the Church, we are the bride. The divine bridegroom "gave himself up" for the bride, who accepted his gift of love and continues to respond through a gift of self.

In reverence to this mystical marriage, Paul proposed a *radical* new call for husbands and wives to be "subject to one another," which ruled out hierarchical distinction. Instead, husbands and wives were instructed to love under one mission—serving Christ—because they were "one flesh." As Paul wrote, "Be subject to one another out of reverence for Christ."[436] He then explained the marital relationship of their shared service according to their masculine and feminine gifts. Paul wrote, "The husband is the head of the wife as Christ is the head of the Church," clarifying that this role required love, sanctity, nourishment, and cherishing. St. Paul's exhortation on the Christian household emphasized

---

[434]   Ibid., no. 11.
[435]   Ibid., no. 7.
[436]   Ephesians 5:21.

four times that "husbands should love their wives."[437] Paul told wives to "*also* be subject in everything to their husbands,"[438] which clearly asserted a "mutual subjection" that was not one-sided.

This relationship must be understood in light of the distinction between men and women, which humanity can't deny any more than nature can allow us to forget. "There develops in humanity itself, in accordance with God's will, the integration of *what is 'masculine' and what is 'feminine',*" as taught by John Paul II.[439] He also pointed out that "*the symbol of the Bridegroom is masculine.* This masculine symbol represents the human aspect of the divine love which God has for Israel, for the Church, and for all people."[440]

Paul saluted, honored, and commended the female disciples who followed Christ, as well as those at Pentecost and deaconesses who served the early Church, such as Phoebe.[441] This honor was not undone by Christ calling *only* men to the priestly service of the apostles, giving them the sacramental charge, the institution of the Eucharist, and the power to forgive sins. The priestly service of the apostles expressed that the relationship between men and women, masculine and feminine, is "willed by God both in the mystery of creation and in the mystery of Redemption."[442]

---

[437]   Ephesians 5:21–33.
[438]   Emphasis added.
[439]   *Mulieris Dignitatem,* no. 7.
[440]   Ibid., no. 25.
[441]   Romans 16:1.
[442]   *Mulieris Dignitatem,* no. 7.

The equal dignity of men and women is affirmed in Christ, who calls both men and women to self-realization through making a gift of themselves. Paul brought this teaching into marriage. He explained how Christ sanctified the roles of husbands and wives (as one body) in marriage according to their masculine and feminine gifts. Wives bring forth new life, educate, and carry burdens alongside their husbands. Husbands love and cherish their wives, sharing in all things with her and protecting her faith and charity, even to the point of sacrificing their lives for hers, as exemplified by Christ. *Mulieris Dignitatem* affirmed that "in the sphere of what is 'human' . . . *'masculinity' and 'femininity' are distinct,* yet at the same time they *complete and explain each other.*"[443]

---

[443]   Ibid., no. 25.

I Am Mother

"That special power of loving that belongs to a woman is seen most clearly when she becomes a mother. Motherhood is the gift of God to women. How grateful we must be to God for this wonderful gift that brings such joy to the whole world, women and men alike! Yet we can destroy this gift of motherhood, especially by the evil of abortion, but also by thinking that other things like jobs or positions are more important than loving, than giving oneself to others. No job, no plans, no possessions, no idea of 'freedom' can take the place of love. So anything that destroys God's gift of motherhood destroys His most precious gift to women—the ability to love as a woman."[444]

—Mother Teresa

I disliked every *physical* aspect of pregnancy: nausea for nine months, aversion to every smell and taste, and somehow hiding a nine-pound child in my small frame. Despite painful sciatica, I often experienced people rushing past me to help women three months less pregnant and three times my size! I prayed through years of healing just to have the *desire* to become a mother, and when that desire came, I

---

[444] Mother Teresa, Talk at the World Conference on Women, Beijing, 1995.

feared not having the right mental tools or spiritual fortitude for motherhood.

I wanted to experience maternal love, which I knew was the greatest gift of my femininity and what had previously seemed unattainable. It didn't matter if that love was biological or spiritual, I just wanted to give a love to others that reflected Divine Love. As I was blessed with children, I realized that my motherhood was the kind of beauty that was written on the face of Mother Teresa: wrinkled, imperfect, and suffering, but what really mattered was the underlying and continuous desire to serve God. The greatest virtue of my motherhood has been love. In one of my favorite messages of Mother Teresa, given at the World Conference on Women in Beijing in 1995, she said, "What I can do, you cannot. What you can do, I cannot. But together we can do something beautiful for God. It is just this way with the differences between women and men."[445] Motherhood, which goes much deeper than its physical dimension, is something my husband can't do. But together, with his gift of fatherhood, we can do something beautiful for God.

The illustrious scholar saint Edith Stein, in 1930, acknowledged the ability of women to fulfill all vocations outside of the priesthood and fatherhood, extending beyond women's original vocation as spouse and mother. While Simone de Beauvoir erroneously stated that "one is not born, but rather becomes, woman," Edith Stein corrected, "No woman is only *woman*; like a man, each has her individual specialty and talent, and this talent gives her the capacity of doing

---

[445]   Ibid.

professional work, be it artistic, scientific, technical, etc."[446] Stein taught women extending themselves into a wider working circle not to be afraid to bring the same spiritual attitude needed by the wife and mother into the workplace. Bringing the feminine nature's specific self-sacrificing attitude, which is concerned with personal elements and looks for concrete goals in adjusting the means to the end, into the public sphere "can become a blessed counterbalance . . . where everybody is in danger of becoming mechanized and losing his humanity," Stein added.[447]

As workplace opportunities continue to became equally available to women, they must strive to preserve their humanity in recognizing the human dignity of others, while cultivating respect for the differing masculine and feminine approaches to education, leadership, and problem-solving. But as Mother Teresa warned, "No job, no plans, no possessions, no idea of 'freedom'" can take the place of a mother's love for her children without destroying motherhood, which is God's "most precious gift to women."[448] Each woman, and more so each mother, has the obligation to conscientiously discern how she is being called to live out her gift of feminine virtue in the world without destroying her motherhood.

Our authentic quest for the true nature of womanhood has been in question since Eve, and it remains a noble quest,

---

[446]   Edith Stein, "The Ethos of Women's Professions," *Essays on Woman*; "The Ethos of Women's Professions" on September 1, 1930 (Washington, DC: ICS Publications, 2017), 49.

[447]   Ibid., 50.

[448]   Mother Teresa, Talk at the World Conference on Women, Beijing, 1995.

regardless of philosophical movements and social revolutions. "Woman" is not solely a product of biology or an internal feeling despite her biology; she is inseparably knit to her feminine soul. She is more than her work, which is sometimes used to define and measure her contribution to society. She is more than her reproductive choices, despite the emphasis feminism has placed on efforts to control conception and termination of children. "Woman" is created to give herself lovingly to others; motherhood is not a worst-case scenario. In a statistical study comparing demographic trends from the 1990s to the 2010s, rates of motherhood in women without advanced education remain at 88 percent, while "highly educated women have experienced particularly dramatic increases in motherhood"—from 65 percent in 1994 to 80 percent in 2014.[449]

Women's Liberation

Women's liberation must begin "with a *universal recognition of the dignity of women*," as St. John Paul II pointed out in his letter to women.[450] Women's voices are louder and clearer today than during the Suffrage Movement and Sexual Revolution thanks to social media and communication advancements. She is not the second sex but the complimentary equal with man in reflecting the divine image of God, and she shares equal responsibility to "transform the face of the earth" beyond science and technology.

---

[449]   A. W. Geiger, Gretchen Livingston, and Kristen Bialik, "6 facts about U.S. moms," *Pew Research Center*, May 8, 2019.

[450]   John Paul II, *Letter of Pope John Paul II to Women*, June 29, 1995.

In *Evangelium Vitae,* St. John Paul II wrote, "In transforming culture so that it supports life, women occupy a place, in thought and action, which is unique and decisive. It depends on them to promote a 'new feminism' which rejects the temptation of imitating models of 'male domination', in order to acknowledge and affirm the true genius of women in every aspect of the life of society, and overcome all discrimination, violence and exploitation."[451]

Feminism has fought an ongoing and divisive battle for co-subjectivity and equality with men. Its prominent attributes are the deconstruction of patriarchy, rebellion against God and nature, and the fight for sexual freedom and reproductive control. Since the turn of the century, modern feminism has adopted the denial of the gender constructs of femininity and masculinity and has reduced maternity to a utilitarian service rather than an act of love. Through these elements, feminism guides women to discover "the antithesis of love" and the perversion of their feminine disposition, which Edith Stein noted "is expressed by vanity, desire for praise and recognition, and an unchecked need for communication . . . curiosity, gossip, and an indiscreet need to penetrate into the intimate life of others."[452] This perversion, though not acknowledged as such, is celebrated across feminist books and magazines and is vastly at odds with the "new feminism" offered by St. John Paul II.

He argues that it is our *femininity* and potential for motherhood that make us, not weak, but distinct. John Paul II

---

[451]   John Paul II, *Evangelium Vitae* (March 25, 1995), no. 99.
[452]   Stein, "Woman's Natural Vocation," 47.

reminds us not to lose sight of Mary and the women who stood with Christ at his crucifixion: "In this most arduous test of faith and fidelity the women proved stronger than the Apostles. In this moment of danger, those who love much succeed in overcoming their fear."[453] The women also loved enough and were fearless enough to first find Christ's empty tomb and to meet and announce the risen Lord. For this act, Mary Magdalene has been called "the apostle of the Apostles."[454] Christ's divine truths were entrusted to women as well as men, thereby proving that our unity in Christ doesn't cancel out our diversity but elevates it.[455]

What Is Femininity?

In the *Letter of Pope John Paul II to Women,* he explained that the special characteristics of collective femininity express a *genius* which authentically enriches human relationships and spiritual values in all areas of human life.[456] This feminine genius bears our spiritual "sensitivity," which is a great feminine strength. It recognizes the deep longing in other human hearts and responds to them in love. Our sensitivity grasps the suffering of others and refuses to allow them to fall victim to an exile on the fringes of society. It's concerned with human beings in every circumstance *because* they are human, and it encourages community.

Our femininity also harbors a special "receptivity," which is no less passive than Mary's response to the archangel

---

453   *Mulieris Dignitatem,* no. 15.
454   Ibid., no. 16.
455   Ibid.
456   John Paul II, *Letter of Pope John Paul II to Women,* June 29, 1995.

Gabriel. Our receptivity is actionable and requires a "fiat" to proceed in love. In *The Privilege of Being a Woman*, Alice von Hildebrand recalled that "authentic creativity in creatures depends upon their degree of receptivity."[457] And yet women, whose bodies are made to receive life, discover a natural ease of heart and spirit through active receptivity. We are naturally equipped to participate in God's authentic creativity.

Our femininity also possesses a special "generosity," motivating us to pour ourselves out for others in our family, community, and in the world. This true generosity protects and centralizes the communion of humanity. It welcomes new life and offers Christian hospitality in order to combat the dehumanization that creeps into society.

But ultimately, it is our *maternity* that is the brilliant culmination of these feminine gifts. Our maternity is inseparable from our self-gift as women. Maternity is our immense capacity to accept others and to thereby bring unity and peace to the human family. As St. John Paul II reminded us in *The Dignity of Women*, we "cannot destroy that readiness to accept life which marks [our] 'ethos' from the 'beginning.'" We are maternal in our nature, soul, and our being. Our femininity is rooted in giving life, and that manifests in many creative ways. We destroy that creativity when we destroy that part of ourselves.

---

[457] Alice von Hildebrand, *The Privilege of Being a Woman* (Sapienta Press, 2002), 64.

Spiritual Motherhood

While the internal process of physical motherhood "involves a special communion with the mystery of life," the spiritual motherhood of women is expressed in nurturing and educating children and others (who are body and spirit). All women possess this potential for spiritual motherhood, which is beautifully exemplified by adoptive mothers, consecrated women, and all women exercising their feminine genius. God introduced motherhood into his covenant through Mary, so that "each and every time that motherhood is repeated in human history, it is always related to the Covenant which God established with the human race through the motherhood of the Mother of God."[458]

Two primary attacks the Catholic Church encounters are made against her defense of the mysteries of celibacy and maternity. In Matthew's Gospel, Jesus said to his disciples that "there are eunuchs who have made themselves eunuchs for the sake of the kingdom of heaven."[459] John Paul II explained that "*celibacy for the kingdom of heaven results not only from a free choice* on the part of man, but also from a special *grace* on the part of God, who calls a particular person to live celibacy."[460] The radical self-gift of being espoused to Christ requires a person to leave everything and follow him. Grace perfects the masculine and feminine natures of the cooperating priest or religious sister through their virginity and spiritual paternity or maternity.

---

458   *Mulieris Dignitatem,* no. 19.
459   Matthew 19:12.
460   *Mulieris Dignitatem,* no. 20.

The Church is also Mother in safeguarding the Christian Apostolic truth and in educating and bringing forth new children through the sacraments into eternal life. The Apostolic Letter *The Dignity of Women* teaches us that the Church maternally harbors "all women as they have come forth from the heart of God in all the beauty and richness of their femininity; as they have been embraced by his eternal love; as, together with men, they are pilgrims on this earth, which is the temporal 'homeland' of all people and is transformed sometimes into a 'valley of tears'."[461]

Her Call to Mission

Edith Stein said, "The deepest longing of a woman's heart is to give herself lovingly, to belong to another, and to possess this other completely." This is femininity. She went on to say, "This longing is revealed in her outlook, personal and all-embracing, which appears to us as specifically feminine."[462] Each of us want to be personally and exclusively loved, even when we fear the commitment and potential for rejection in returning that love. Our body and soul yearn to love and be loved. Women's bodies are *made* to harbor others. But beyond that, women express love in a deeply spiritual way (each in her own way), welcoming other souls to unfold within her love, as Edith Stein so beautifully put it.

When I rejected and devalued my gift of self, I also became selfish. I couldn't nurture my own heart and refused

---

[461]   Ibid., no. 31.

[462]   Edith Stein, "The Supernatural Vocation of Woman" on September 1, 1930, *Essays on Woman* (Washington, D.C.: ICS Publications, 2017), 53.

to allow my Creator in. I also began to believe the lie that I was unlovable and had no love to offer others. As Alice von Hildebrand defended in her talk "The War on the Supernatural," we cannot understand the mystery of femininity without supernatural enlightenment.[463] A war is being waged on life by those expanding the abortion initiative, seeking to label motherhood as a disease and pitting women against their irreplaceable feminine genius, which is sorely needed in today's world. Don't be afraid! As St. Paul said in his letter to the Romans, "Do not be conformed to this world but be transformed by the renewal of your mind, that you may prove what is the will of God, what is good and acceptable and perfect."[464]

Femininity doesn't mean living out our holiness in the same way as other women. It has been displayed in many exemplary ways throughout history by those women who have followed Christ and worked to bring communion to the human family. Some have dedicated their lives to prayer and service, while others have led Christocentric movements for justice. The greatest model is the Mother of God. Femininity universally shares the gift of maternal love. Through our maternal love, women distinctly reflect one of the two images of God in our equal humanity with men. We will lose the battle—and ourselves—in the process of trying to recreate ourselves as men, or by renouncing gender entirely. But by bringing into the world all that God intends through our full cooperation with him, we will participate in his

---

[463]   Alice von Hildebrand, "The War on the Supernatural," Human Life International Audio CD.

[464]   Romans 12:2.

divine creation and renewal; our lives, and the world, will be richer for it.

The true nature of womanhood is etched into the deep wrinkles of the feminine soul. It is that radical, objective radiance that delights the soul to such a depth of shining clarity that it moves others to embrace its divine source. Actively embrace your feminine genius and fight for a culture that ushers in life, bears witness to genuine love, and creates authentic relationships, while upholding the dignity of every human person. Be receptive to the good gifts God desires to give you and sensitive to the marginalized: the unborn, the poor, the oppressed and abandoned. Be generous in pouring yourself out to others and in sharing the fullness of all that you've received. Let your maternal love shine in sharing a love that is life-giving.

Acknowledgments

Padre Pio said, "My past, O Lord, to Your mercy; my present, to Your love; my future to Your providence." This book is a testimony to the love of Christ in my life and is written in great thanksgiving to those who have walked with me through it. I'm thankful to my beloved parents and brother and to all those who have loved and encouraged me to pursue truth, beauty, and goodness. To Kevin Keane, Charles and Mary Piccirilli, Pam and Ken Stachiw, and to the New Life Community. In great thanksgiving for my teachers, friends, and the friars at the Franciscan University of Steubenville, as well as the Sacrifice of Love Household. To Fr. Thomas Petri and the friars at the Dominican House of Studies in DC and the community at Christendom Graduate School in Virginia.

In enduring love and thanksgiving to my husband Cory, our beautiful children (who interrupted me a million times with hugs and kisses and funny stories), and our supportive families. In special gratitude to Monica Hortobagyi Siniff, for her tireless help with this project. For the guiding support of Fr. Anthony Sortino and the encouragement of Fr. Thomas Vander Woude. In gratitude to Dr. Donald Asci, Dr. David Crawford, Craig Turner, Dr. Carrie Gress, Emily Ricci, Matthew Horne, and Dr. Alice von Hildebrand for their contributions to this project.

In gratitude to TAN Books, and especially John Moorehouse, Conor Gallagher, and Geri Addamo for believing in me. Thanks to Marjorie Dannenfelser, Dr. John Bruchalski, and Kathleen de Habsbourg-Lorraine. I am forever grateful and humbled by the support of the many others who have encouraged me, endorsed this work, and those whose hearts share its message. You are loved!

About the Author

Kimberly Cook is a writer and the host of the popular podcast *The Dignity of Women*. Her marriage workbook, *My Hand in Yours, Our Hands in His,* earned her the Catholic Writers Guild Seal of Approval in 2018. She is co-author of *Into the Wilderness: 40 Day Devotional for Catholic Single Women* and *Once I Was Blind, But Now I See.* Kimberly was one of the featured experts on the documentary *From Eve to Mary: The True Dignity of Women,* and her work regularly appears on Catholic news and journalism sites. Kimberly holds an MA in systematic theology and a BS in mental health and human services. She runs KimberlyCook.ME, an outlet for thought and discussion on reclaiming femininity and challenging modern feminism. Cook lives in Virginia with her husband and children.